England's

HISTORIC
GARDENS

A TEMPLAR BOOK
Copyright © 1989 by Templar Publishing Ltd
All photographs copyright © John Bethell, except pages
54, 123, 141, 142 (bottom left), 143 (top right) and 144
copyright © Christopher Thacker

First published in Great Britain in 1989
by HEADLINE BOOK PUBLISHING PLC

British Library Cataloguing in Publication Data
Thacker, Christopher
England's historic gardens: an illustrated account of one
nation's garden heritage
1. England. Gardens
I. Title
712'.6'0942

ISBN 0-7472-0110-2

This book was devised and produced by Templar
Publishing Ltd, Pippbrook Mill, London Road,
Dorking, Surrey RH4 1JE

Editor: Caroline Ball
House editor: Amanda Wood
Designers: Mike Jolley & Mike Blacker
Typesetting: Servis Filmsetting Ltd, Manchester

Colour separations by La Cromolito, Milan, Italy
Printing and binding by New Interlitho, Milan, Italy

England's HISTORIC GARDENS

by CHRISTOPHER THACKER

Photographs by JOHN BETHELL

HEADLINE

CONTENTS

• • •

*'Landscape with lake – and mansion':
the northern view towards Castle
Howard, completed in 1795–9 when
the Great Lake was created.*

• • •

FOREWORD

*By Lord Montagu of Beaulieu
Chairman of English Heritage*

• • •

*T*his splendid book written by Dr Thacker and conceived and illustrated by photographs by John Bethell, has captured the aesthetic appeal of this quintessentially English work of art – the garden. All its richness and diversity is here too – ancient and modern, architecture and plantsmanship, peaceful and bizarre. Valuable service is performed whenever gardens are presented so attractively, with the motivating ideas behind them explained so well, and I am thus delighted to be providing this foreword.

I would like to include a few words about the Register of Parks and Gardens and Dr Thacker himself. During the 1970s and early 1980s the idea of a Register was floated by the Garden History Society and other groups. Lists were drawn up for a few counties, but the process was protracted by being through voluntary effort alone. A permissive power in the National Heritage Act of 1983 fortunately allowed English Heritage to take this work on professionally, which it did, with the help of Dr Thacker. Some county lists were nearly in a publishable state, but the great bulk of the work was still to be done. Only someone of Dr Thacker's knowledge and perseverance could have undertaken the task. Nigh on 1100 properties were described, allocated to grades and the resulting lists published in three years of prodigious effort.

Just as Dr Thacker's work was coming to a close, the Great Storm of 16 October, 1987, devastated south-east England. A great tragedy, but one that English Heritage was able to respond to. Consultants were sent out to gardens on the Register in the affected areas. Quite soon we had a clear picture of the scale of damage and were able to ask the government for funds to mount a grant scheme for help with repairs. Unless we had had the Register at hand we would have been poorly placed to take such action. A sad emergency yes, but one that dramatically proved the importance of the Register. Every day, I am assured, it continues to prove its value in the face of local plans, planning applications and highway proposals.

Sadly, gardens decay even when protected; they are a perishable art form. We must therefore renew and restore our gardens if they are to continue to be of historic and aesthetic value. Restoration grants for gardens are presently available from English Heritage only in the limited case of storm damage repair. One hopes, though, that we will find ourselves in a position to be of assistance more widely in the future – a useful complement to the advice we provide already. This is a concern and an activity we share with the County Gardens Trusts – now, I am glad to say, increasing in numbers. English Heritage has welcomed these Trusts and looks forward to mutual co-operation in the future.

If this book helps to foster an appreciation of what it is that we and the voluntary bodies are striving to keep, it will prove itself a worthy sequel to the Register. Thanks must go to Dr Thacker for having provided us with both, and to John Bethell for this visual record.

An evening view north towards the castle at Hever, looking down a walk flanked with rhododendrons from the hillside above the Golden Stairs.

• • •

Montagu of Beaulieu

28 February 1989

INTRODUCTION
• • •

*I*n the beginning – or as near as makes no difference – was the garden. And straight away it began to change. While the oldest gardens and parks described in this book – Windsor Great Park, for example, or Knole or Hyde Park – have grown or shrunk, altering their boundaries, and have changed in character with families and fashions, with periods of expansion or neglect, and with successive good or bad seasons; while these venerable places have changed, so too have the more modern gardens described, even the most recent, East Lambrook Manor, not begun until 1939–40. The 'great' storm of October 1987 was not the first, nor will it be the last, to flatten whole landscapes of trees; and since that storm, those battered landscapes are changing again, with new trees growing in place of the old.

John Bethell's photographs, taken in the last couple of seasons, are therefore as close to an up-to-date record as one could hope, as are the English Heritage *Registers of Parks and Gardens of special historic interest in England*, which I was engaged to compile from 1984 to 1988.

These Registers, one for each county in England, provide succinct descriptions of the present characteristics and historic aspects of nearly 1200 of England's parks and gardens, and are the first full survey of this part of our historic heritage. Rather in the manner of a little 'Domesday Book', the Registers list and describe *what is here now*. They are – like John Bethell's photographs – a statement that these gardens exist, and that they are, in many and glorious ways, places of interest, beauty and incalculable value.

In the Registers, the gardens and parks were allocated 'grades' according to their importance and quality (Grade I, the highest, followed by Grade II*, and then by Grade II). The gardens described and illustrated in this book are virtually all listed in the Registers as Grade I, and they provide a marvellous scheme of reference for a book which aims to present the changing panorama of England's historic gardens. As a point of interest, the concern of the Register was with gardens and parks which had 'historic features dating from 1939 or earlier'. While many of these pre-1939 gardens and parks

contained later features which were mentioned (such as the conservatories opened at Kew in the last couple of years), gardens created entirely since 1939 were not included. This will of course change in later editions of the Registers.

Work for the Registers began in 1983, following the requirements of the National Heritage Act 1983, para. 10, Schedule 4. An advisory committee drew up preliminary county lists of gardens and parks, and compilation of the Registers began in 1984. Assistance with the information came from many sources, most notably from the owners and occupiers of the gardens, who were consulted before publication; from local planning authorities, and also from interested organizations such as the National Trust, the Garden History Society, and the Centre for the Conservation of Historic Parks and Gardens, the University of York. This help is gratefully acknowledged in the Introduction to the Registers.

The parks and gardens described here are in a wide variety of ownership. Four are administered by English Heritage – Audley End, Belsay, Osborne and Wrest Park; twenty-three by the National Trust – Belton, Biddulph, Claremont, Cliveden, Clumber, Dunster Castle, Farnborough Hall, Hardwick, Hidcote, Kedleston, Knole, Montacute, Packwood, Petworth, Rievaulx Terrace, Scotney, Sheffield Park, Shugborough, Sissinghurst, Stourhead, Studley Royal, West Wycombe, Wimpole. The rest are either Crown or public property, or in private or institutional hands, and are not necessarily 'open to the public'.

Though the vast majority of these parks and gardens are open to the public, at least on one or two days a year, some are entirely private. This book aims to describe 'England's historic gardens', but is *not* a list or gazetteer of gardens to visit. There are several handbooks produced regularly with details of 'houses and gardens open', such as *Historic Houses, Castles and Gardens open to the Public*; *Gardens of England and Wales* (the 'Yellow Book'); the respective handbooks of the National Trust and English Heritage; and further lists of local interest, and I suggest that you consult the appropriate handbook to see *if* and *when* a visit may be allowed.

Top: The medieval castle at Warwick once had small formal gardens close to the castle mound, but these were swept away by Capability Brown in 1749; then, in 1868–9, Robert Marnock introduced striking floral features near to the castle – the five-sided parterre garden, and this, the rose garden, which has been thoroughly restored in 1985–6.

Bottom left: Salvin's imposing mansion at Thoresby was built in the 1860s, and the formal terraced garden there is probably his work as well. Stone-edged beds are typical of much Victorian formal garden design.

Bottom right: Massed bedding, in a superb geometrical arrangement – and in full mid-Victorian style — in the Italian Garden at Mount Edgcumbe. This strongly architectural feature, with balustrade, steps and sculpture facing a central fountain, has been here since 1799.

• • •

Chapter One

IN THE BEGINNING

• • •

*O*ur word 'paradise' goes back to the Persian, to the word *pairidaeza*, meaning an enclosure, which was applied to the enclosed hunting park of the great king. It is one of the earliest words used to define the idea of the park or extensive garden, and while its later history – through Old Testament Hebrew and through Greek – led to its religious sense, 'the abode of the blessed', the enclosed hunting parks to which it first referred remain to this day as one of the oldest and most long-lived of garden forms.

In England we have scores of old parks which were enclosed – emparked or empaled – in the Middle Ages, in order to preserve deer for hunting, and not a few survive with deer in them today. The oldest – such as Windsor Great Park, of which a part was enclosed by 1086, and the present area of some 5600 acres achieved by about 1365 – are at least of Norman origin. Others might claim to be older still, having evidence that they were already in existence at the time of the Conquest – we may think of Godinton Park in Kent, where the venerable trunk of an oak recorded in Domesday lies in open ground not far from the present house. Others were clearly enclosed by the later Middle Ages: Hackwood by 1280, Highclere and Stonor of similar date. When the first building at Penshurst Place was made in the early fourteenth century, it was accompanied by a deer park. Drayton House has a medieval deer park dating from 1328.

The lake and deer park at Hardwick Hall are part of the early history of this site, brought to its glory by Bess of Hardwick's mansion, 'more glass than wall'.

• • •

Above: Richmond Park was enclosed in 1637, and has held deer ever since. Now crossed by public roads and footpaths, its 2500 acres contain many woodland areas and numerous recreational features.

• • •

By the fifteenth century, such parks were widespread. There was a deer park at Greenwich from 1433 – the highest part of the present Greenwich Park, to the south, still bears the name, though there are now only about 30 deer. The 1000-acre deer park at Knole was established in this period, and today boasts herds of fallow and Japanese deer – and a golf course. In the 1500s came a score of others, including Hampton Court for Cardinal Wolsey, Hyde Park for Henry VIII, Chatsworth and Hardwick (the last, in the 1590s). By 1617 Fynes Moryson could write

No nation of great compass alloweth such great proportions of lands for Parkes to impale fallow or red Deere. And as England hath plenty of red Deere, so I will boldly say, that England (yea perhaps one County thereof) hath more fallow Deere then all Europe that I have seene.

Virtually all of these deer parks have changed since their first enclosure. If they have survived (and hundreds have not) their boundaries have been enlarged, or reduced; they have had different houses built in different areas; and they have most often been returned in part to agriculture or forestry – or worse.

But this has not always been characteristic. One of the most impressive of the surviving deer parks in England is at Helmingham Hall, where the parkland contains scattered oaks of immense size and age. Medieval fishponds near St Mary's church are passed to one side by an early eighteenth-century avenue of oaks leading to the moated house. The parkland was 'landscaped' in the 1760s, with a mound or 'mount', and in the early 1800s Constable came to sketch an oak tree in the Dell, a mile north of the Hall.

THE WALLED GARDEN

While 'paradise' is linked to the idea of the enclosure of the hunting park, our word 'garden' goes back to an enclosure of a smaller kind (it is cognate with both 'garth' and 'yard'). The *garden* began as an enclosure, for vegetables or fruit trees, usually near to the house, and enclosed with a quickset hedge or a fence, or a wall in grander establishments. Whether hedge or fence or wall, this was needed to keep animals – and robbers – out, and tended to give a geometrical outline to the area which often influenced the sub-divisions of the garden, making them square or rectangular in turn.

Though many deer parks survive – with or without deer – the smaller garden enclosures which were made in the Middle Ages are much less easy to show, since their original garden content has disappeared. True, the walls are still there, in many a cathedral or abbey cloister, or beside a castle or medieval manor. But within those walls there is now nothing to say how a small medieval garden may have been. It is proper to be firm about this. No medieval gardens (apart from their walls) survive, whether in England or in western Europe as a whole. While the architecture is there in splendid completion – go for example to St Trophime, at Arles, in France – the original centre (the garden) is desperately absent, replaced by grass and pathetic bedding. Whatever may have been planted there in the Middle Ages, or in the sixteenth century, has gone, and we must not deceive ourselves that in this or that religious or secular quadrangle the *planting*, the

vegetation, is other than of a later age. In England we have, alas!, no small gardens older than, say, the early 1600s, though the occasional tree may be older than the surrounding scheme.

Again and again, however, we may see the walls, the framework, the 'skeleton', and magnificent these architectural remains may be – such as the walls, with semi-circular buttresses, built at Mells Manor House for Abbot Richard Beere of Glastonbury in the 1520s, or the various remnants of monastic walls at Newstead Abbey, some possibly from the thirteenth century, and the rectangular Eagle Pond with its surrounding terraces. Extensive walled gardens were made for secular dwellings – as at Stonor, where parts of the garden walls may go back to the original twelfth-century manor house, though they are mainly from the Tudor period. At Parham, the walled garden covers some five acres, and dates from the building of the house in 1577. The quadrant layout is thought to have been maintained since the garden was first designed.

Grandest in this category are the great walls enclosing the dwellings at Knole and at Penshurst Place. In each instance the walls are as much fortifications as garden enclosures – at Knole, they include an area of some 27 acres, at Penshurst Place 11 acres. At Knole they were begun in the mid-fifteenth century, and their fabric dates mostly from the later sixteenth century. Their main divisions have probably been kept since Tudor times, though there is no firm indication of the layout until the late seventeenth century, when several wrought-iron gates were set in the walls marking the place of the main paths or avenues. At Penshurst, the walls were built between 1570 and 1666, and, as at Knole, the present layout was probably established in its main lines in that period.

Above: In the ancient park at Helmingham – the view over the medieval fishponds (the Leys), looking towards the Hall. The causeway leads to the church of St Mary.

• • •

13

HELMINGHAM HALL

• • •

*T*he oaks in the park at Helmingham Hall are of immense age, and may be among the oldest trees in the country. It is not certain when the park was enclosed (it now holds both red and fallow deer), though it is probable that the original area was enlarged, first in the seventeenth, and again in the eighteenth century, and the fine 350-yard avenue of oaks from the Hall to the south-east was planted around 1700. Landscaping in the mid-eighteenth century added a mound or mount half a mile to the west, now surmounted by an obelisk, erected in 1860. In the Dell, roughly a mile to the north-west of Helmingham Hall, is the oak which Constable sketched in 1800, and twice painted – in 1826 and around 1830 – as 'Helmingham Dell'.

The Hall stands within a square moat, and its fabric dates from the mid-sixteenth century, remodelled in the eighteenth and nineteenth centuries. To the south-west, a separate rectangular moat encloses $4\frac{1}{2}$ acres of walled and formal gardens. While the date of this moated area is not known with certainty, it may go back to the early Middle Ages. The present walls, dated 1749, enclose a layout which has been little changed for two centuries. The present outstanding planting of flowers and shrubs, both *within* the walled garden, and round the *outside* of the moated walls, originated in the later nineteenth century, and has been brilliantly developed in the last decade. Recent features outside the moat include a meadow garden, to the south-west, and a herb and knot garden on the far, outer side of the Hall moat.

Above: Helmingham
Hall – with the moat in
front, and topiary.

Left: From the Hall,
itself contained in a
separate moat, the
moated garden and its
divisions can be seen
most clearly. The moat,
with water lilies, in the
foreground extends right
round the outer side of
the far garden walls.

Far left: The
Tollemache crest rises
over the entrance gate to
the walled garden. While
the walls bear the date
1749, the moated garden
enclosure is far older.
The herbaceous borders,
among the finest in the
country, have been
renowned at
Helmingham Hall since
the late nineteenth
century.

. . .

While Knole and Penshurst are instantly impressive by their size, the walled garden at Helmingham Hall is fascinating for its rarity, being moated, and separate from the moated house which it adjoins. The moated garden enclosure, of 4½ acres, is thought to date from the fifteenth century, though its present walls were built in 1749, and the division of the main area into eight parts in the eighteenth century has since been simplified to a scheme of four quarters.

Within these walled enclosures, as I have said, no ornamental planting schemes remain from the time of Elizabeth or before. They have gone, yet since the mid-nineteenth century many attempts have been made to replace them, based on information, plans and illustrations which appeared in gardening and topographical works from the mid-sixteenth century onwards, the first being Thomas Hill's *Most Briefe and Pleasant Treatyse* of 1563. The knots, the mazes, the elaborate topiary, the joke fountains, the complex yet ephemeral trellis-work structures known as 'carpenter's work' are recorded in many descriptions and illustrations, and the continuing interest in their re-creation is in itself a fascinating aspect of garden history.

While the many varieties of knots which adorned the gardens and quadrangles of Oxford and Cambridge colleges have gone, they lingered longer than elsewhere. William Gilpin describes the intricate figures which he saw at New College, Oxford, as late as 1742:

In one . . . you may discover his Majesty's arms cut out of box, in the opposite one they have done as much for the Founder of their College, in a third, you have a figure of a sundial made of the same materials, which answers to a fourth clipt out into the form of a Labyrinth.

The mound (or artificial hillock) which stood behind these four knots is still there. It was begun in 1529–30, though not completed until 1648–9, with fine stone steps and a viewing platform at the top. Today, it is tree-clad, overlooking a lawn where once the knots had been laid out – and where joyous plays are put on in the summer term. Oxford still retains two other garden features of great antiquity: the college walks at Magdalen, beside the Cherwell, and in Christ Church meadows. These tree-lined walks are already marked on the Agas map of Oxford of 1578, and may be compared with the walks along the Backs at Cambridge, beside the Cam. Addison's Walk at Magdalen is named after Joseph Addison, a Fellow of the College, whose essays in the *Spectator* did so

much to promote the love of nature – and the birth of the landscape garden – in the early eighteenth century. But these and the related Water Walks at Magdalen were already famous by Addison's day – in 1691, Anthony Wood wrote in *Athenae Oxonienses*:

> Go into the Water-walks, and at some times of the year you will find them as delectable as the banks of Eurotas, which were shaded by bay trees, and where Apollo himself was wont to walk and sing his lays.

Unlike the gardens within the quadrangles, these walks have changed but little since Elizabeth's reign. In 1911, Max Beerbohm wrote, in *Zuleika Dobson*, of Christ Church meadows 'the scent of these meadows' moisture is the scent of Oxford. Even in hottest noon, one feels that the sun has not dried *them*'.

SLEEPING BEAUTIES

Many of these garden frameworks were of course greatly modified in later years. This was the case at Hampton Court, where Wolsey's and then Henry VIII's extravagant walled enclosures to the north of the palace, and a smaller garden to the south (the Privy Garden, beside the Thames), were largely remodelled or removed in the following century, first for Charles II, and then for William III. Many stretches of wall remain, particularly in the Tiltyard and Wilderness areas to the north. To the south, the Banqueting House was built around 1700 on the site of a Tudor garden tower.

In Derbyshire both Haddon Hall and Hardwick Hall have kept fine garden structures from the late sixteenth century, in part because they were neglected, or at least disregarded for long periods. Haddon Hall, begun in the twelfth century and much enlarged and remodelled around 1600, and given a wonderful series of terraces with steps and balustrades at this time, is one of the 'Sleeping Beauty' gardens of England, since from 1701 until 1912 it was rarely used by its owners, the Dukes of Rutland. Already in 1697 Celia Fiennes had noted that it had 'good Gardens but nothing very curious as the mode now is' – in other words, she thought they were old-fashioned. Preserved but little used for two centuries, Haddon Hall and its gardens were at length restored from 1912 onwards – a task which took the 9th Duke of Rutland some 25 years. Somewhat in the same way, Hardwick Hall, built between 1591 and 1597 for Bess of Hardwick, the dowager Countess of Shrewsbury, and given a fine framework

Below: At Haddon Hall, the superb terraces beside the house were built at the end of the sixteenth century, with parapet, balustrade and stairs. Their present planting is from the first half of the twentieth century, a part of the long restoration of the Hall and its gardens by the 9th Duke of Rutland. This view is of the fine rose garden on the upper terrace.

• • •

of garden walls, lodges and garden houses, was allowed to 'slumber' for long periods, and was first given an exuberant garden renovation in the 1870s by Lady Louisa Egerton, and a second restoration by the National Trust after 1959. All that remains of the sixteenth-century planting at Hardwick is paradoxically *within* the house, in the astonishing collection of eight-sided embroidery panels, depicting herbs, flowers and plants illustrated in Mattioli's *Herbal* of 1568.

The spacious framework at Montacute has a similar history. Designed when the house was built, 1590–1601, the main areas of Upper Garden, Forecourt, Terrace and Lower Garden were vigorously refashioned in the mid-nineteenth century (a mount in the centre of the Lower Garden was replaced in 1894 by a balustraded pool and fountain). Gertrude Jekyll commented in 1904, in *Some English Gardens*: 'It is all extremely correct, stately – dare one say a trifle dull?' But the twin pavilions at the outer angles of the Forecourt are among the glories of Renaissance garden architecture, and the borders beside them are a part of the National Trust's thoughtful planting since the 1950s.

To my mind the garden framework whose content – both of plants and Renaissance waterworks – I should most like to have seen preserved is that at Hatfield House. The plans for the gardens were drawn up in 1609 by Mountain Jennings for Robert Cecil, later 1st Earl of Salisbury, and in 1611 waterworks were designed by the Huguenot Salomon de Caus. The planting was directed by John Tradescant (the Elder, *c.* 1570–1638) – of whom more must be said shortly. But these gardens, just like those at Hardwick, Haddon or Montacute, have gone, and the outstanding and varied features there today are largely the creation of the nineteenth century – such as the great maze, laid out in 1841 – or the later twentieth century, like the knot garden laid out in 1980–1 beside the east front of the Old Palace.

THE SEVENTEENTH CENTURY

Moving on into the seventeenth century, we begin to find garden features which are still, to some extent, as they were first created. So at Woburn Abbey, there is the strictly architectural grotto made in the north range of the house around 1627, and attributed to Isaac de Caus (Salomon's nephew). In 1697 Celia Fiennes describes three large separate gardens round the house: 'fine gravell walks and full of fruite – I eate a great quantety of the Red Coralina goosbery which is a large thin skin'd sweete goosebery' – admiring mainly the rare plants, and the statue of 'an old weeder woman . . . which is done so like and her clothes so well that at first I tooke it to be a real living body'. But, apart from the grotto – now used as a most elegant refreshment room – all gone.

> I accompanied Mr. *Howard* to his Villa at *Alburie*, where I designed for him the plat for his Canale and Garden, with a Crypta thro the hill &c.

So wrote John Evelyn in September 1667. Already in August 1655 he had noted in his diary that Mr Howard (Thomas Howard, 2nd Earl of Arundel) had begun to 'alter the Gardens much'. At last in September 1670, he added

> to *Alburie* to see how that Garden proceeded, which I found exactly don according to the Designe and plot I had made, with the *Crypta* through the mountaine in the park . . . such a *Pausilippe* is no where in England besides.

Evelyn's work at Albury is, we may think, the last creation of a garden in the spirit of the Renaissance – attempting to make something comparable to the great Italian gardens of the sixteenth century, with their extravagant terraces and waterworks, all adorned with classical sculptures, and consciously commemorating the sites, monuments and history of ancient Greece and Rome. Today, two 400-yard-long terraces from Evelyn's design remain. In the centre of the upper one is a semi-circular arcaded bay, overlooking a pool. This bay forms the entrance to the *Crypta*, alluding to the grotto of Sejanus at Pausilippo, and leads to a 150-yard-long tunnel through the hillside. Below, the lower terrace has a central doorway leading to an underground bath-house. Evelyn's scheme included a long rectangular canal below the terraces, but this was drained in 1920. In the early 1920s, the surrounding grounds were markedly changed in character with the planting of a great variety of trees, many of which are now mature.

It is frustrating to be given snippet after snippet about the marvels of these vanished gardens, and so, to do for all, a single quotation may be allowed, from John Taylor (the 'Water Poet'), who wrote in his *New Discovery* in 1623 describing the gardens at Wilton made earlier in the century by the gardener, Adrian Gilbert, for the 3rd Earl of Pembroke. Gilbert had

used such a deal of intricate setting, grafting, planting, inoculating, railing, hedging, plashing, turning . . . and every way curiously and chargeably conceited; there hath he made walks, hedges and arbours, of all manner of most delicate fruit trees . . . resembling both divine and moral remembrances, as three arbours standing in a triangle, having each a recourse to a greater Arbour in the midst, resembleth three in one and one in three; and he hath there planted certain Walks and Arbours all with Fruit trees, so pleasing and ravishing to the sense, that he calls it *Paradise*, in which he plays the part of a true *Adamist*, continually toiling and tilling . . .

Right: 'If Wholesome Air, Earth, Woods, and pleasant Springs Are Elements, whereby a house is grac'd: Such is the house of Wilton, *and so plac'd' wrote John Taylor in 1623. Wilton's changing gardens have continued to elicit admiration. Since 1737, their principal ornament has been the Palladian bridge.*

• • •

All gone, all gone – swept away this time by Isaac de Caus, who redesigned the entire garden scheme in the 1630s, fully illustrated in his book *Wilton Gardens*, published around 1640. It was an integrated layout, proceeding regularly down a central axis aligned on the garden front of the house. In this respect it must have been one of the first gardens in England in the new French (rather than Italian) style, with the entire scheme of *parterres* and lesser garden areas subordinated to a central, house-orientated design. At the far end was a grotto – this still inspired by Italian examples – with statuary, waterworks and joke fountains. In the 1690s, Celia Fiennes could admire the 'many fine figures of the Goddesses', and the several pipes which could 'wet the Company . . . at the Artists pleasure'. There were also musical effects – 'it makes the melody of Nightingerlls and all sorts of birds' – with attendant wettings.

Grotto and gardens lasted until the early eighteenth century, though in diminishing glory. In the 1730s the area was landscaped for the 9th Earl of Pembroke, who himself designed the Palladian bridge, in cooperation with Roger Morris. It was built in 1737 across the little river Nadder, and is a landmark, both physically in the garden, and in the development of the English landscape garden as a whole, uniting the admiration for notable architecture with admiration for the scenery and natural landscape in which it is set.

THE PLANT HUNTERS

'In the beginning' there were also plants – but in England (before the great period of Tudor exploration, which coincided with the upsurg-ing curiosity about the world, past and present, which we call the Renaissance) the native species were not anything like as numerous as we may think today, looking over our well-stocked and kaleidoscopically varied gardens. A part of the spirit of enquiry of the Renaissance was directed to the flora and fauna of the natural world, and in 1543 and 1545 the botanic gardens of Pisa and Padua were founded to collect and preserve the plants, known and recently discovered, from the Old World and the New. In England, this enthusiasm was quickly adopted, and collections of plants, and books about them, were made from the mid-sixteenth century onwards. At Syon Park, a botanic garden was established for the Duke of Somerset by Dr William Turner (*c.* 1508–68), who compiled a herbal, the first to be written in English and to include descriptions of native species. His small catalogue, in English, *The Names of Herbs*, was published in 1548. At Syon, a clump of red mulberries (*Morus nigra*, introduced from Persia around 1500) is thought to have been planted by Turner.

Turner was followed by other writers and collectors – John Gerard (1545–1612) produced a catalogue of over 1000 species collected in his own garden, at Holborn, in 1596, and his *Herball* was printed the year after; John Parkinson (1567–1650) had a garden at Long Acre, and produced his *Paradisi in sole* in 1629. By this time, John Tradescant the Elder had been involved at Hatfield for the Earl of Salisbury (from around 1611 to 1614), as well as at other notable gardens, and in 1618 he travelled to Russia, in 1620–1 to coastal parts of north Africa, and in 1627 to France. The illustrated manuscript of 'Tradescant's Orchard', now at Oxford in the Bodleian Library, has coloured

drawings of many different fruits which he is thought to have cultivated at Hatfield. His own, and his son's garden at Lambeth, was famous for its collection of rare plants.

While these private garden collections have gone, two public or institutional gardens from the seventeenth century survive. The first, the Oxford Botanic Garden, was founded in 1621 by Henry Danvers, the Earl of Danby. The surviving walls and imposing gateways are by Nicholas Stone, and were built in 1632–5. It is important to note that the original four-part division of the garden was intended – like that at Padua – to receive the plants from the world's four continents, Europe, Asia, Africa and *America*, a concept unimaginable before Columbus's discovery of the New World in 1492.

This book is concerned with the history of England's great gardens, not with the history of England's plants and trees, native or introduced from abroad. It is none the less essential to note some of the many successful introductions to England (many of them to western Europe as a whole) which were made in the sixteenth and seventeenth centuries. These plants or trees come not only (like the potato, the tomato and the tobacco plant) from the New World, but from Persia, Turkey, the Middle East or the Balkans:

Holm oak, or evergreen oak (*c.* 1500); Red Mulberry (*c.* 1500); Arbutus or Strawberry tree (before 1548); Stone pine (1548); African marigold (*Tagetes erecta*, *c.* 1550); Tulip (*c.* 1578); Crown imperial (*c.* 1580); Hyacinth (*c.* 1580); Oriental plane (*c.* 1582); Yucca (1593); Laburnum (before 1596); Laurustinus (before 1597); Sunflower (before 1597); Nasturtium (before 1597); Lobelia (before 1627); Passion flower (before 1629); Horse chestnut (1637); Swamp cypress (1640); Cedar of Lebanon (by 1659).

Oxford University's Botanic Garden is the oldest in Britain – in October 1664 Evelyn was there, observing 'two large *Locust* [or Carob] *Trees*, and as many *Platana*, and some rare plants under the culture of old *Bobart*'. Jacob Bobart was the first keeper, and published the first plant catalogue in 1648.

Much later in the century comes the Chelsea Physic Garden, founded in 1673 by the Worshipful Company of Apothecaries. Intended, like the Oxford Botanic Garden, as a teaching institution, its layout was geometrical, with subdivisions into small rectangular beds – *pulvilli* in Latin – which could conveniently be observed by students. Though the original layout was much amended in the 1890s, some areas of these beds have been retained, with plants arranged in systematic order – as they may still be seen at old botanic gardens on the Continent, such as Padua, or Leiden, or Uppsala, or at the new university botanic garden at Düsseldorf.

The Chelsea Physic Garden was quickly renowned. Its greatest benefactor, Sir Hans Sloane, has his statue, erected in 1748, at the junction of the main axes, and Philip Miller (1691–1771) was keeper from 1722 for nearly fifty years, producing the many editions of his *Gardeners Dictionary* in this period. In 1772, Joseph Banks brought back to the Physic Garden some 40 tons of volcanic lava from Iceland, which now form the nucleus of the first European habitat designed for rock plants.

Botany has its enthralling moments – and its longueurs. In May 1712, Dr Ralph Thoresby recorded in his diary that, in company with the great garden designer George London

they drilled me on to the Physic-garden at Chelsea, where their lectures on the exotic plants were amusing; but detained us too long, that though we returned by water, had not time to wash, that I appeared shamefully like a sloven at dinner . . .

Above left: Founded in 1673, the Chelsea Physic Garden was originally and remains in essence a teaching institution, for the study of plants and their medicinal properties. The groups of small, rectangular beds enable plants to be examined closely, and have been characteristic of botanic and physic gardens since the Renaissance.

Above: Modern floral borders in front of Nicholas Stone's gateway to the University Botanic Garden at Oxford, built in 1632–5. Founded in 1621, the Botanic Garden is the oldest in Britain, but much younger than those at Pisa or Padua, founded in 1543 and 1545. Yet its purpose was the same – to receive, to study, and to disseminate plants from all quarters of the world.

• • •

Chapter Two

TO SUIT WITH VERSAILLES

• • •

*T*o understand the gardens created in England in the late seventeenth century we must look to France – and nowhere else. Louis XIV, *majesté très-chrétienne*, was supreme as political, military and cultural dictator throughout western Europe. His gardens at Versailles had been developed from the 1660s with the intention of impressing all comers with his omnipotence. From the centre of the great palace – in the end, some 400 yards across – the gardens extended westwards through the half mile of the *Petit Parc* to another mile of the Great Canal – along a central axis which said, more than anything else: 'This leads through the garden of my palace, where I, *le Roi Soleil*, the Sun King, reside'. Each part of the gigantic scheme – miles of forest-rides, a vast central cross-shaped canal, separate residences at Trianon and the Ménagerie, and the multiple *bosquets*, tree-enclosed garden features of sculpture, fountains and pavilions, of the *Petit Parc* – each part was subordinated to the one idea of the king's authority. Here, unruly nature had been tamed – hedges clipped to a green geometry, stone carved into elegant statues, and water forced to spout and spray and gush in exuberant yet always rigidly controlled patterns. Seeing the fountains at Versailles, the poet Delille wrote that Man might exclaim proudly: 'C'est moi qui créai ces prodiges' – '*I* made these marvels'. They were indeed man-made, but they were made *to order*, for one man – Louis XIV. The spirit of Louis XIV's gardens was imitated throughout Europe. Other rulers, great or

Laid out in 1689 by the French gardener Guillaume Beaumont, the gardens at Levens Hall now contain topiary forms of unique interest and diversity.

• • •

small, made similar gardens and parks, extending the architectural 'authority' of their palaces out over the countryside. These gardens survive, some intact, some as outlines of vanished grandeur, from Russia and Sweden to Italy and Spain, from Austria to the Netherlands – and to England.

England was in fact one of the first countries to receive Louis's message, and with reason. Charles II was first cousin to Louis XIV, and had been his guest in France during the period of Cromwellian rule. Returning to England in 1660, he began in the following year to have a great formal garden made at Hampton Court, and to have the ground at St James's Park, between Buckingham House and Whitehall, laid out with a formal canal, the tree-lined avenue of the Mall running along the northern boundary. Edmund Waller celebrated the latter in verse, 'On St James's Park as lately improved by His Majesty' (1661), writing of the formal planting on each side of the canal:

> For future shade, young trees upon the
> banks
> Of the new stream appear in even ranks.

While St James's Park today retains little of its original French inspiration, being drastically, and marvellously, remodelled by Nash in 1828–9, Charles II's work at Hampton Court survives in grandiose outline, having been much elaborated for William III from 1689 onwards.

Charles II's garden activities in 1661 provide a curious parallel with those of Louis XIV in France, who began his prodigious expansion at Versailles in the early 1660s. Charles II had asked Louis XIV if his great garden designer, André Le Nôtre (1613–1700) might be allowed to cross the Channel to redesign St James's Park. But this did not happen – indeed Le Nôtre is known to have supplied only one design for an English garden, at Greenwich in the 1660s, and it is likely that he did not ever visit the British Isles. Even at Greenwich the main formal layout for the park may have been devised not by Le Nôtre but by André Mollet, who executed several commissions in England.

CHANGES OF A NEW REIGN

Hampton Court is the first great garden of the seventeenth century which we can see in England in something like its original form. As already noted, the great deer park, together with that of Bushy Park to the north, was created in the early sixteenth century for Cardinal Wolsey, followed by Henry VIII, as were the gardens adjoining the palace. The remodelling of the garden areas has continued into the present century, as fashions have come and gone, and as the years go by we may expect more changes within the great framework. This is a part of what gardens 'are about'; yet if we are fortunate, as at Hampton Court, much of the seventeenth-century garden will always be preserved.

Its main French-inspired layout was begun in 1661–2, with the excavation of the Long Water, the long rectilinear canal which leads away eastwards from the semi-circle of gardens on the east side of the palace. The French garden

expert André Mollet (d.c. 1665) has been suggested as Charles' designer, though the plan was laid out by Adrian May. How elaborate the gardens were at this time is uncertain – in June 1662 John Evelyn was there, and commented that the park, 'formerly a flat, naked piece of Ground', was 'now planted with sweete rows of *lime-trees*', and the canal was 'for water now neere perfected'. Yet he adds that 'all these Gardens might be exceedingly improved, as being too narrow for such a Palace'.

Another Frenchman, Guillaume Beaumont (d. 1727, and best known for his work at Levens Hall), was active in the area of the Wilderness (the earlier Great Orchard of Henry VIII's garden) in the late 1680s, and then, from 1689 onwards, the entire scheme was brought to perfection, after the accession of William III.

In the late 1680s, in the troubled years round the end of James II's reign and the beginning of William III's, the diary of John Evelyn makes gloomy reading. Garden enthusiast that he was, his notes at this time are almost wholly to do with the political and military crises surrounding the Revolution of 1688. Then suddenly, in July 1689, a brief entry reads

16th. I went to Hampton Court about business, the Council being there. A great apartment and spacious garden with fountains was beginning in the park at the head of the canal.

Left: Little remains of the seventeenth-century St James's Park, the lake and paths being given their sinuous form by John Nash in 1828–9, and the 'landscaping' also given gently undulating contours. Thanks to these curving lines, the park is able to contain large numbers of visitors without appearing desperately crowded. It might seem to be the prototype of many later urban parks, aiming to give a sense of the countryside – in the heart of Whitehall.

• • •

HAMPTON COURT

• • •

*H*ampton Court represents England's 'equivalent to Versailles' more than any other garden in the country, with its great semi-circular Fountain Garden before the palace, extended by the Long Water. These features, developed by Charles II and William III, followed park and garden activity at Hampton Court since the early 1500s, closely linked to the development of Bushy Park to the north.

While the garden layouts of Cardinal Wolsey and Henry VIII are now visible only in the form of enclosing walls, the Fountain Garden and Long Water firmly retain their formal outlines, inspired by the gardens of Louis XIV. Yet here, as in many other parts of the park and gardens, varying influences from later periods have had a permanent effect – most notable being the superb displays of floral and foliage bedding, many in proudly Victorian style, and some from the present century. These appear in beds set in the grass of the Fountain Garden, and in the several small formal garden areas – the Pond Gardens – between the Privy Garden and the Great Vine. The extended herbaceous bedding along the Broad Walk is one of the most magnificent examples of its kind.

In the area of the Wilderness, the Maze, laid out after 1689, is an extraordinary survival, when considered beside the twentieth-century rose gardens, the laburnum walk, the lawns, spring bulbs and shrubbery. I hope the Maze is immortal – and that we may long remember Harris's words in Jerome K. Jerome's *Three Men in a Boat*: 'You keep on taking the first turning to the right. We'll just walk round for ten minutes and then go and get some lunch.'

Right: *The Great Vine, 'planted in the year 1769 . . . from a cutting [of a Black Hamburg] taken from a large plant at Valentine House in Essex'. The planting is attributed to Capability Brown, and the vine is still astonishingly prolific, 'bearing bunches in almost incredible numbers'.*

• • •

Left: There are today no finer displays of flower and foliage bedding than at Hampton Court. This brilliant combination might well have been laid out at some point in the gardens at any time since the 1850s.

Below: The small formal gardens to the side of the palace have been drastically redeveloped in this century. The Banqueting House beyond was built on the site of a Tudor viewing platform.

• • •

Above: Bushy Park's fine avenues were laid out in 1689–99, linked to the layout of Hampton Court. The statue on the Diana Fountain, by Fanelli, was brought here in 1713, after an earlier siting in the Privy Garden beside the Palace. It represents Arethusa, not Diana – but what's in a name? The circular basin had been made around 1699.

• • •

It is, we may think, a turning-point. It marks, as neatly as any single snippet can do, the first cultural act of the new reign – and it involves gardening. Some years later, Daniel Defoe will write in his *Tour through the Whole Island of Great Britain* (vol. 1, 1724) that 'it is since the Revolution that our British gentlemen, began so universaly, to adorn their gardens with those plants, we call ever greens' – and this 'strange passion', as he terms it, he attributes to William himself:

> the king on his part introduc'd . . . the love of gardening . . . his majesty was particularly delighted with the decoration of ever greens, as the greatest addition to the beauty of a garden, preserving the figure of the place, even in the roughest part of an inclement and tempestuous winter.

King William's 'love of gardening' was clear enough, with his works at Het Loo and Hampton Court. Yet we must not be misled by the tercentenary excitements in 1988 into believing that there was such a thing as an 'Anglo–Dutch' garden. While the generally level, and canal-drained terrain of the Netherlands led to the modification of plans 'to suit with Versailles' (George London's phrase, in relation to Melbourne), the overall conception of these gardens remained firmly aligned on the meridian of Versailles, and most of the garden designers were French, or had been to Versailles, and met Le Nôtre. In England, William's love of gardening appears principally at Hampton Court, and with a firmness of purpose which is still apparent through the changes brought by later centuries.

While Sir Christopher Wren developed and enlarged the Palace, giving classical coherence to the long garden front, George London (d. 1714) developed the semi-circular Fountain Garden (the Great Parterre) in front of Wren's façade, using an embroidery parterre design by Daniel Marot, the Huguenot émigré who had earlier worked for Louis XIV at Marly, near Versailles, and then for William of Orange at Het Loo in the Netherlands. Another French émigré, Jean Tijou, made the great wrought-iron screens for the gardens in about 1689. London also covered the Wilderness area with a formal layout, of which the most interesting element to survive is the Maze, in the north-west corner, and laid out a separate parterre to the south of the palace, on the site of Henry VIII's Privy Garden. This design, enlarged around

1700, has since been submerged in nineteenth-century shrubbery, but there is talk of change . . .

George London's work at Hampton Court continued until the early eighteenth century, and extended far into the surrounding parkland – across into Bushy Park, where the Chestnut Avenue, aligned on the Lion Gates (in the north wall of the Wilderness at Hampton Court), stretches northwards for a mile to join the Lime Avenue at the Diana Fountain (basin *c.* 1699, with statue added in 1713).

LONDON AND WISE

George London (*c.* 1650–1714) has been named as a principal designer of the gardens at Hampton Court, and his name, with that of Henry Wise (1653–1738) will recur in the following pages. In 1681, George London was a junior partner in the newly founded Brompton Park nursery (with Roger Looker, Moses Cook and John Field), and Wise was also a partner by 1687. By the 1690s the concern was supplying a large number of plants and young trees to gardens in many parts of the country, Wise superintending the running of the nursery, while London travelled widely, dealing both with orders of plants and trees, and with the design and layout of gardens. He travelled abroad as well, going to France in his younger years with his early master John Rose, the royal gardener; to the Netherlands in 1685; and to France again for some six months in 1698 to study French gardening methods in Versailles, when he is thought to have met the aged Le Nôtre.

IN THE FRENCH MANNER

While it is easy to single out Hampton Court as the most important garden scheme to be developed under French influence, it is difficult to separate the crowd of English gardens in the French style into 'early' or 'late' examples, since many of them were begun in the reigns of Charles II (1660–85) or James II (1685–8), and then further developed in the reign of William III (1688–1702), while others retained characteristics from still earlier periods, which were modified to bring them into line with the fashion for greater formality.

The complexity of garden politics in the 1680s is a problem. Not a few gardens were begun, with enthusiasm, *before* the affairs of 1688. At that point, some landowners withdrew to their country properties and 'gardened' there since they were no longer acceptable at Court; others developed their country properties, since they had become Court favourites. There are therefore many gardens in this period which may be termed 'pro' or 'anti' William. Their style, however, remains French.

Such complexities embrace the walled garden enclosures in Kent of Knole and Penshurst, built long before the troubles of the 1688s. At Knole the walls are mainly from the later sixteenth century, to which wrought-iron gates from the late seventeenth century were added, while the surviving subdivisions of the 27-acre gardens were largely established (by Thomas Acres or Akres) in 1710–11; at Penshurst Place, the walled enclosure (11 acres) was built between 1570 and 1666, and the present layout has been essentially the same since the late seven-teenth century. Individual features, and the planting, have of course changed immensely in both gardens in the last century.

Greenwich – emparked in 1433, with a fence round some 200 acres – was given a brick wall round the park in 1619–24, shortly after the Queen's House was begun by Inigo Jones. After the formal, and possibly French, layout in the 1660s, Christopher Wren built the Royal Observatory (Flamsteed House) in 1675–6 on the spur of the high ground southwards from the Queen's House, and it was from the terrace viewpoint here (adorned since 1930 with the statue of General Wolfe) that he claimed the necessity for a garden on the other, northern side of the Thames, as a conclusion to the view from Greenwich, and as a superb point from which Greenwich itself might be viewed. *This garden, named the Island Gardens, was opened – at last – in 1895 'amid great enthusiasm'.*

Below: Greenwich Park shares a history of honourable complexity with other royal parks, such as Hampton Court or Windsor Great Park. This view looks across the site of the 'Giant Steps', laid out in the 1660s, to the Royal Observatory (Flamsteed House), built by Wren in 1675–6.

• • •

PENSHURST
PLACE

• • •

*W*ithin the medieval park, the 11-acre walled enclosure of the house and gardens at Penshurst Place was built between 1570 and 1666, and its formal division into quarters and lesser sections has remained constant since the late seventeenth century. There is a general similarity in this respect between Penshurst Place and Knole, though in details the two gardens diverge considerably.

Neglected in the eighteenth century, the gardens were restored in the 1850s, and given a grand parterre with strongly defined box-edged compartments. A century later, from 1945 onwards, the gardens have been again developed with enthusiasm and imagination, many eastern areas (within the walled enclosure) being adapted from their previous use as orchard or vegetable and soft fruit regions, while retaining a great many of the old fruit trees.

Writing about these gardens in 1904, Gertrude Jekyll gave high praise to the herbaceous borders established in the later nineteenth century, and to 'the fine taste and knowledge of garden effect with which they have been used'. This 'fine taste' she explained, was due to the alternation of bright colour – the borders – with less vivid areas:

> There are not flowers everywhere, but between the flowery portions of the garden are quiet green spaces that rest and refresh the eye.

This statement has equal force at Penshurst Place today, with grassy orchard groves beside the herbaceous borders, and garden enclosures with gentle colour tones such as the Silver Garden (developed in the 1970s) alternating with scenes of vivid colour.

Above: The deer park at Penshurst Place was enclosed in the Middle Ages. Still standing beside the lake is the Sidney oak, thought to be of medieval origin. In modern contrast is the double poplar avenue, planted in 1965, and leading south for 400 yards towards Penshurst Place and the great walled garden.

Left: The Italian Garden was laid out by George Devey around 1850, on the site of the late seventeenth-century parterre. Devey's main plan has been retained ever since, with varied planting in the box-edged bedding areas. These have recently been replanted with roses.

Far left: Within the walled gardens at Penshurst the ground slopes gently down from west to east, allowing interesting changes of level between the different areas. This border of paeonies leads to steps, rising up to the Italian Garden. In the background are some of the garden's many aged apple trees.

• • •

Bottom right: The gardens and park surrounding Boughton House are among the most important examples of a large formal scheme to survive from the late seventeenth century. The Broad Walk extends westwards from the house, from the terrace overlooking the site of formal parterres down to the lake, connected by canals to further garden features developed by around 1700.

• • •

More wholly created under the French influence were Cliveden, Longleat, Boughton and Chatsworth. At Cliveden, on a raised bluff overlooking the Thames (Evelyn called it 'that stupendous natural rock'), 'august and stately' gardens were made in the late 1670s below William Winde's mansion. It is not known who designed these gardens – possibly Winde himself. In 1696 the Cliveden estate was acquired by Lord George Hamilton, who became Earl of Orkney soon after. In 1713 he commissioned several new parterre designs, from Claude Desgots (Le Nôtre's nephew) and from Henry Wise, but settled on a much plainer design of lawn and terrace. The Cliveden layout and the surrounding grounds went through considerable development by Charles Bridgeman around 1723, before the immense re-creation of the Cliveden landscape in the nineteenth century.

Longleat – which we think of now as a great sixteenth-century house within a far later *landscape* – had (and we may add 'of course', for a mansion of such magnificence) its original garden scheme, which was maintained well into the seventeenth century, shown in Jan Siebe-rechts' painting of 1675. From 1682 a formal scheme by London and Wise overlaid the earlier layout, and was completed by 1694, involving parterres, bowling green, labyrinth and fountains. This too was to be largely obliterated with the advent of Capability Brown.

At Boughton, the spacious scheme which survives today may still be traced in part to its origins in the mid-1680s, when Ralph, 1st Duke of Montagu, who had been Ambassador to France until 1669, had formal gardens laid out beside the house (itself in French style. Defoe wrote in 1725 that it was 'very much after the model of the Palace of Versailles'). Montagu's gardener was a Dutchman, Van der Meulen, and he worked at Boughton until the death of the 1st Duke in 1709.

By Defoe's time the gardens and park had been enlarged by the 2nd Duke, who added further avenues to those begun by his father. Boughton is one of the most notable geometrical 'canal' gardens of England, with a spreading network of canals and pools, approached or flanked by triumphant avenues – chestnut, beech and lime going back to 1715 or before. Westwards from the house, the terrace is adorned with mid-eighteenth-century lead vases by Roubiliac, and looks out over the great lawn (site of the original parterres) to the Broad Water, and beyond, along the Broad Walk, to the horizon. South of the Broad Water is an artificial 'mount', beside which the canal leads towards the Star Pond and Cascade, dating from about 1700. These were restored in 1976.

Chatsworth has as rich and complex a garden history as anywhere in England, and its several periods of glory must compete with each other for pre-eminence. While the first gardens went back to the fifteenth and sixteenth centuries (the raised garden-cum-viewing platform of Queen Mary's Bower, 1570, still stands in the parkland by the river Derwent), the main gardens of Chatsworth were begun in the mid-1680s, like those at Boughton. Vast formal gardens (120 acres) were laid out on the side of the valley to accompany the substantial remodellings of the house which took place from about 1676 to 1680 and again between 1686 and 1707. George London was the principal garden designer, setting out parterres, a bowling green, a greenhouse, pools with fountains, including C.G. Cibber's Seahorse Fountain, and areas of clipped hedges and topiary walks. The Frenchman Nicolas Huet worked on the terraces.

Contemporaries were particularly struck by the contrast between the sumptuous elegance of the gardens, and the rough moorland which surrounded the valley of the Derwent. Defoe called the hillside 'a waste and houling wilderness', where one looked down 'from a frightful heigth, and a comfortless, barren . . . and endless moor, into the most delightfull valley, with the most pleasant garden, and most beautiful palace in the world'. That this contrast is not felt with any such force today is due to the work of Capability Brown in the later eighteenth century.

Within the seventeenth-century gardens the most striking feature was the Cascade, designed by another Frenchman, Grillet, in 1694 or 1695, and imitating the *Rivière*, the gigantic step cascade at Louis XIV's Marly. Within three or four years it was extended, and by 1703 had been given Thomas Archer's fine cascade house at the summit. Not that all was grand and solemn. Nearby was a 'Grove' with 'a fine Willow tree, the leaves barke and all looks very naturall . . . and all on a sudden by turning a sluce it raines from each leafe and from the branches like a shower'. Celia Fiennes also saw 'a bason in which are the branches of two Hartichocks Leaves which weeps at the end of each leafe', and Dr C. Leigh, writing in 1700, saw 'another pond, in which is an artificial rose,

32

Left: Unlike the house, the gardens at Longleat display little of their sixteenth-century origins. This formal garden area, between the house and the orangery, was noted in the mid- and later nineteenth century for its displays of massed bedding. While the fine architectural outlines of hedges and pool have been retained, the planting is now simpler – and more delicate.

• • •

Above: While the 'River' – the great step cascade in Louis XIV's garden at Marly – has gone, the imitative cascade at Chatsworth, begun in 1694 or 1695, survives triumphantly. The Cascade House is by Thomas Archer, who also designed the Banqueting House at Wrest Park.

• • •

by turning of a cock the water ascends through it, and hangs suspended in the air in the figure of that flower'. The original joke fountains have gone, but the Willow Tree was replaced in the nineteenth century, and its sprinkling showers may still be enjoyed.

'ROWES AND WALKES OF TREES'

It must not be thought that 'formal' means 'uniform' in garden design. Though later advocates of 'natural' landscaping were to attack the old gardens for a soul-destroying symmetry – as Pope wrote in 1731:

'Grove nods at Grove, each Alley has a
    Brother,
And half the Platform just reflects the
    other'

– there was a wonderful variety between the outstanding examples of the formal style. It was due sometimes to accidental differences of site – Chatsworth within a hilly region, Hampton

Court on level ground - but as often to deliberate differences of emphasis in the garden scheme. At Badminton, the great formal avenues laid out by London and Wise in the 1690s for the Duke of Beaufort still subsist in partial magnificence, after considerable restoration in the 1970s. These avenues, radiating from the house, were originally intended to lead each to a separate parish church in the outlying countryside. Celia Fiennes wrote in 1698 that 'you may stand on the leads and look 12 wayes down to the parishes and grounds beyond all thro' glides or visto of trees'. Nearer to the house were parterres, lawns with fountains, a bowling green and a clipped formal 'wilderness', which have since been obscured by eighteenth-century landscaping and replaced by nineteenth-century flower gardens.

Avenues were also praised at Drayton House, in Northamptonshire – the Great Avenue southwards from the house remains, with substantial replanting. In 1763 Horace Walpole noted that the parish church was 'at the end of

an avenue about a mile from the house', and he also admired the gardens closer to the house for their old-fashioned formality (like the house itself – 'there is scarce a House in England so entire in the old-fashioned manner'). They retained 'a mall', like the Mall on the north side of St James's Park, for the French game of *le mail*; and 'cradle walks with windows cut in them, just as it was made by Sir John Germain, who brought the taste from Holland'.

Great avenues were also laid out at Althorp. The main avenue today leads northwards away from the house; Evelyn noted 'the rowes and walkes of Trees' in August 1688, with a garden 'exquisitely planted and kept'. This formal framework was reinforced in the 1860s when W.M. Teulon laid out a balustraded bedding scheme to the north and west of the house. Other grand avenues were planted at Stansted Park in the late seventeenth century, and the main beech avenue still stretches eastwards from the house – its length as great as any other in the country.

THE TOPIARIST'S ART

If Badminton or Stansted were notable for avenues, Levens Hall and Packwood have become noted for their topiary. Levens Hall and its surrounding deer park have medieval origins, but the building was remodelled considerably in the sixteenth century, and at several later dates. In the late seventeenth century, long avenues were laid out in the park, and some ten acres of formal gardens were developed round the Hall. A Frenchman, Guillaume Beaumont (who had worked earlier at Hampton Court), was responsible for the layout and planting, begun in 1689 and completed by the end of the century. No one would doubt that the original scheme of parterres, clipped hedges and trees was intended to have the balance and regularity inherent in any garden designed in French formal style, but in its subsequent growth the topiary work has achieved such individuality that it is unique in Europe as a late-seventeenth-century survival. It must have been neglected –

Above: One of the grandest avenues in the country – the great beech avenue at Stansted Park, laid out with other formal features in the late seventeenth century. It may be compared with the Broad Avenue in Cirencester Park, developed from about 1714 onwards.

• • •

Right: *The assembled topiary at Packwood House, said since the late nineteenth century to represent the Sermon on the Mount, is of uncertain origin, and may, like Topsy, or the topiary at Levens Hall, have 'just growed', during a period of neglect. At Packwood, the main topiary yews around the Mount were there by 1756, and may be considerably older.*

Far right: *The U-shaped canal at Chicheley Hall was laid out in 1700–1 by George London, enclosing lawn and parterres in front of the house. This three-sided water feature is a rare survival from the period when gardens were made 'to suit with Versailles'.*

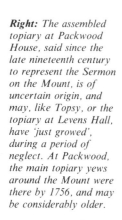

• • •

or, in other words, 'allowed to grow' – at some point, probably in the eighteenth century, like the now huge conical yews in the semi-circle at Hampton Court (of which Thomas Jefferson wrote laconically in 1786: '*Hampton-Court. –* Old fashioned. – Clipt yews grown wild').

We might wonder what M. Beaumont would say of his creation, could he see it today. The striking, and sometimes bizarre, topiary shapes are certainly cared for with skill and devotion, and have since the late nineteenth century had a thoughtful underplanting of contrasting annuals. In 1904 the head gardener at Levens Hall, W. Gibson, singled out *Lobelia cardinalis* and *Salvia patens* as 'far more effective than others when planted among yews'. They 'should be largely grown in every garden where there are a lot of yews' (*The Book of Topiary*, by C.H. Curtis and W. Gibson). M. Beaumont would approve the lobelia – it had been introduced to England (via France) from North America in the 1620s – but the salvia would surprise him. It was not introduced, from Mexico, until 1838!

We may imagine that the monumental topiary at Packwood House had a somewhat similar origin, though its beginnings are less clearly known than at Levens. Packwood House dates mainly from the mid-sixteenth century, and the adjacent garden areas are from the mid- and later seventeenth century, including the small Roman Bath of 1680, one of the gazebos, and the wrought-iron gate (1675) in

the south garden wall. Then, in the early eighteenth century, the area south of the house was given another corner gazebo and the curious 'bee-boles', or beehive-shaped recesses, in the southern wall, while the topiary garden was set out on rising ground further to the south, with a 'mount' at the far end. The central plantings of yews round the mount, and along the central avenue, are known to have been there before 1756, while lesser specimens to the sides were added after 1850. Their present size, and closeness together, suggest that their original purpose may have been less spectacular. Since the late nineteenth century, the tall, clustering and slightly rounded shapes have been said to represent the Sermon on the Mount, with Apostles and Multitude listening to the words of Christ.

GRAND DESIGNS

By the 1690s the French style in gardening was immensely popular, and many gardens bore the marks of this enthusiasm. At Stowe, the first signs of the great layout to come appear in a sketch of the 1690s, and in Celia Fiennes' comments around 1694 on the 'visto thro' the whole house, so that on the one side you view the gardens which are below one another with low breast walls and terrace walks . . . on the other side you see the parke rowes of trees'. By

1700, work had begun at Chicheley Hall on avenues in the parkland, and in 1700–1 on a three-sided (or U-shaped) canal opposite the garden front of the house, enclosing twin embroidery parterres and lawns with pyramid yews. The designer was George London, who had also designed formal gardens before the south front of Grimsthorpe Castle and avenues in the park around 1690. In 1700 or thereabouts Thomas Coke of Melbourne Hall had likewise chosen a plan for his garden, sent to him by London and Wise, which they said was 'to suit with Versailles'. We may assume that their claim was true, since London had spent around six months at Versailles in 1698. The chosen plan for Melbourne was executed from 1704 onwards.

While the early formal garden at Stowe was to be wholly submerged in grander developments, the water-scheme at Chicheley survives round a spacious lawn, with eighteenth-century features and later plantings in the grounds. At Grimsthorpe, London's parterres became the site of an elaborate Italianate scheme in the nineteenth century, whose simplified outline is still maintained. Stretches of London's long approach avenues may still be seen, though affected by later landscaping.

At Melbourne, however, his scheme 'to suit with Versailles' survives with its main lines intact. An earlier garden laid out on falling ground to the east of the house was remodelled

to form a small but perfect pattern, with twin parterres by the house, followed by a terrace and lawns, and completed at the foot of the slope by a symmetrical pool, the Great Basin. The parterres were later replaced by lawn. By 1706, the vista down the main axis from house to pool was terminated by Robert Bakewell's Iron Arbour, one of the most distinctive and delightful of all summerhouses. To the south of the pool a further area of ten acres was laid out around 1704 as a formal woodland garden, with

Below: The walled kitchen garden at Grimsthorpe Castle was given its present layout in 1965, to a design by Lady Ancaster.

• • •

a sequence of intersecting *allées* connected by *rond-points*, some with sculpture, others with circular pools. This fine scheme likewise survives, with clipped yew hedges and lime walks, and numerous lead figures by J. Van Nost supplied in 1700–5, including the sumptuous vase of the Four Seasons, at the centre of the main *rond-point*, and the far smaller sets of *amorini* placed beside the parterres.

Like so many of the great English gardens, Wrest Park is astonishing in its historic complexity – a fact one might not gather at first sight from the garden terrace. The centuries-old mansion at Wrest was partly rebuilt in the 1670s, and by the mid-1680s work on the park to the north and gardens to the south had been started. The main garden southwards was created from about 1702 to 1705, with matching parterres and fountains, and two mazes, aligned on the house, and leading to a straight canal – the Long Water. The design may have been by Thomas Acres, who was also designing gardens at Knole in 1710–11. By 1709 or 1711 the vista down the Long Water had been completed by Thomas Archer's Banqueting House. Though this scheme was simplified by the 1730s, and the canal was reshaped at its northern end, and though Capability Brown later made extensive changes to the encircling woodland, the essen-tial vista has been maintained. It was in fact given extra force in the mid-1830s, when the old house was demolished, being replaced by a new mansion designed in part by the owner, the 2nd Earl de Grey, and sited 250 yards further to the north. This made space for an entirely new nineteenth-century parterre, with a grand geometrical scheme of bedding and clipped bushes round groups of statuary; and it is from the garden terrace of Earl de Grey's mansion that we now look out over Victorian bedding and statuary, to the Long Water and Archer's serene pavilion nearly half a mile away.

A PALACE FOR A HERO

'*Wise* and *London* are our heroick Poets', wrote Addison in the *Spectator* of 6 September 1712. He had been explaining that there were many forms of gardening, not just one. And on the 'heroick' scale, these practitioners (by this time the most experienced garden designers in the country) had laid out several versions of 'an agreeable mixture of Garden and Forest, which represent everywhere an artificial Rudeness', which Addison admired in the great gardens of France and Italy (*Spectator*, 25 June 1712). Their grandest scheme was at Blenheim, where – in cooperation with Vanbrugh the architect

Right: 'Thames, Thames, you will never forgive me!' Brown exclaimed when he created the broad lake at Blenheim round Vanbrugh's monumental bridge. He was not rivalling the great river, but stopping the modest flow of its tributary, the little river Glyme, from reaching the Thames.

• • •

who designed the palace and the bridge – the garden and parkland were laid out from about 1705 onwards. It is a sign of the continuing strength of the 'aesthetic of Versailles' that this huge work, paid for by the nation in gratitude to the Duke of Marlborough for his triumph over the French at the battle of Blenheim in 1704, should in many respects attempt simply to outdo the grandeur of Louis XIV's palace and gardens. While Vanbrugh's curious architectural style may be seen as a departure from classical forms, the character of the gardens is severely geometrical: an immense parterre set on a 'bastioned' emplacement, with an enormous vista into the park on the other side, stretching from palace to forecourt to bridge to avenue – some three miles in all. There is also a gigantic and surviving 'bastioned' kitchen garden, eight acres in size. The avenue is flanked by rigidly symmetrical plantings of trees. While Wise's parterre was swept away by Brown in the 1760s, his avenue, punctuated by Townesend's Column of Victory (1727–30), still stands and flourishes, the regular plantings of trees having been renewed in 1902 and 1978–80. Between the

avenue and the palace, Vanbrugh's Palladian bridge is of course still there, but in an immeasurably different setting. Defoe, in 1725, wrote tartly of the regal palace built for a private citizen. Only the aim of creating 'a national building' could 'vindicate' the size and expense of the palace, and this applied with equal force to the 'vast design' of the bridge, 'of one arch costing 20000*l.* and this . . . without a river'. 'Without a river' was an exaggeration. The tiny river Glyme – eight, ten feet wide at the most – trickled underneath, and its disproportion was quickly apparent. 'That damn'd bridge', as Sarah, Duchess of Marlborough called it, was near to ridiculous. By 1720, steps were taken to make the river look more important, but it was not until Brown was called in that the present landscape was created, producing a harmony of bridge and water which Vanbrugh and Wise had never imagined.

One feature Vanbrugh did imagine, but it was too 'advanced' for his patrons. In 1709, he proposed that the parkland beyond the little river and the bridge should be allowed to retain the ruined fabric of Old Woodstock Manor.

Above: Vanbrugh's great bridge now seems perfectly sited – as if it crosses the lake at the one sensible place.

• • •

39

This, he said, would save much money, since the site when cleared would remain as 'an Irregular, Ragged Ungovernable Hill, the Deformitys of which are not to be cured *but by a Vast Expence*'; and, far more important in his reasoning, the ruin was of strong historic interest, being the 'Ancient Remains' of 'Rosamonds Bower' and could easily make 'One of the most Agreable Objects that the best of Landskip Painters can invent'. Vanbrugh's suggestion was turned down. But it was not long before ruins, historic associations, and the visions of the landscape painter were to be all the rage and among the most highly valued elements of the landscape garden. In his further involvement with garden architecture – notably at Castle Howard and at Claremont – Vanbrugh himself was to further the 'historic' cause.

One of those who came to work with Wise at Blenheim was Stephen Switzer. In 1711 he followed George London at Grimsthorpe, extending the 1690s' parterre scheme southwards by cutting a radial pattern of avenues through the adjacent wood, and enclosing this woodland area with a boundary walk, wall and outer ditch. At each of the points where the radial avenues reached the wall there was a protruding bastion, so that the wood seemed to be enclosed by a 'fortification', like Wise's great parterre at Blenheim. Though the bastions have gone, the wood at Grimsthorpe is still there, overlooking the park.

WOODLAND WALKS

In 1699 or 1700, Thomas Archer designed a new house at Bramham for Robert Benson, who had just bought the 611-acre estate in Yorkshire. The layout of gardens and park followed by about 1710, was much developed in 1727–8, and adorned with temples and monuments around 1750. Though a parterre was laid out south-west of the house (since replaced by a formal rose garden), the principal features then, as now, were the extensive walks or rides in undulating woodland, and for the most part these were not aligned directly on the house – an early and fascinating deviation from the authoritarian and residence-centred garden tradition of the previous half-century. The principal alignment, the Broad Walk, runs parallel to the garden front of the house, from the Ionic Temple (by James Paine, 1750-62), past the house to the Obelisk Pond and cas-

cades, and far on to the Rotunda, *c.* 1750, and Obelisk, 1768, in the woodland of Black Fen.

In 1728 the Great Reservoir was constructed, partly to allow a further supply of water for the cascade, and partly as a striking water feature in its own right. Called the T Canal, the longer arm of the water is aligned on the house some 300 yards away, the shorter arm on the Four Faces monument to the west, and on a *rond-point* in Black Fen to the east. Close to the shorter arm is the Gothic Temple, 1750, itself aligned with Obelisk Pond. Further woodland rides or walks link these and other monuments, and are joined to a raised walk laid out in 1727–8 round much of the outer boundary of the gardens – an early example of a ha-ha terrace, and symptomatic of the interest in views of 'natural' countryside which had by then developed.

I have stressed the importance of the connected scheme of *allées* at Bramham Park, since – as Christopher Hussey pointed out in *English Gardens and Landscapes* – 'its nature can, and always could, only be grasped *ambulando*, by progressing through it'. How hugely different from the central vistas or Versailles, or Hampton Court – or even of Melbourne!

The central vista was certainly a part of the great formal scheme at Stowe, which was enlarged from its modest though Versailles-orientated beginnings in the 1690s from about 1714 onwards for Sir Richard Temple (later Viscount Cobham). The new garden designer was Charles Bridgeman, while the garden buildings were designed by Sir John Vanbrugh, and by James Gibbs and William Kent after 1726. Bridgeman had trained under Henry Wise, and may have worked as draughtsman for Wise at Blenheim from around 1713. He was active in many garden developments in the early eighteenth century, his work being for the most part still firmly formal in character – like the immense double avenue of elms (now replanted with limes), $2\frac{1}{4}$ miles long, which he laid out at Wimpole in the early 1720s.

Bridgeman's garden scheme south of the house was centred on the main southern axis, and on areas to the west connected by straight avenues, and with various garden buildings at intersections or completing the vista. This main axis stretched away from the house, through grassed terraces, a pool, and clipped hedges and trellis-work with statues on either side, down to the Octagon Pool (with central Guglio, an obelisk spouting water from each of its four sides), with flanking Lake Temples, and on

Above: The great 'canal' at Shotover, made soon after 1718, and not unworthy of comparison with similar features at Versailles or Chantilly, yet the 'wind of change' was blowing, and few such formal water features were made again in England.

Right: For over a century the cascade and canal at Stanway House have been drained, but the steps of the cascade have recently been excavated.

Far right: At St Paul's Walden Bury, the formality of the diamond-shaped layout of avenues is given a gentle and astonishing beauty by the grassy paths between the long clipped hedges. The Lake Temple, by Sir William Chambers (c. 1770), was added in 1961, being brought from Danson Hill in Kent.

• • •

To the north of the house, the half-mile approach drive from the west arrived at an equestrian statue of George I, by Van Nost, and then turned to the house, past a rectangular canal.

While the gardens at Stowe which we see today retain parts (and essential parts at that) from Bridgeman's design, their appearance was to be changed (if not transformed!) in the next few decades, particularly through the work of William Kent – a matter to be discussed in the next chapter.

At Shotover, the house is as French in style as Boughton. It was built in 1718 for James Tyrell, and soon afterwards given a splendid straight canal on the eastern side, stretching out for half a mile, to rival the Long Water at Hampton Court. In aesthetic terms, it does better, thanks in part to the slope of the ground. It is the grandest formal water prospect in England. At the far, eastern end of the canal the view is completed by the Gothic Pavilion, built possibly by the 1720s, though it may be somewhat later. This building is a three-arched 'temple' with castellated pediment and flanking turrets. The arches are slightly pointed, and the building as a whole is reminiscent of the outer views of the Codrington Library at All Souls, built by the Oxford master mason William Townesend in 1716. With this building, as with the ha-ha walls at Blenheim, Stowe and Bramham, we move well into the new interests of the eighteenth century. At Shotover, gardens on the other side of the house (to the west) were developed by William Kent in the 1730s, with an octagonal temple and an obelisk, though their dating is uncertain.

The medieval deer park at Stanway was given formal gardens round the house in the seventeenth century – these are shown in Atkyns' engraved view of 1712 – but in the early eighteenth century these were partly replaced, on the eastern side of Stanway House, by a canal raised on a terrace some 100 yards away from the house, and fed by an impressive cascade, coming from the higher ground further to the east. There were six stone waterfalls along the cascade, which was fed from an artificial pool above, concealed by the Pyramid, a square tower with pyramidal top, erected in 1750. It has a magnificent view westwards, over the house. The cascade and its canal have both gone – the canal was drained by 1850 – but the terrace retains the name 'Canal', and the stonework of the cascade has recently been uncovered.

towards Buckingham. The main features to survive from this period are Vanbrugh's Rotunda, built by 1724, and William Kent's first architectural contribution, the Temple of Venus, built c. 1730–1 on a bastion at the south-western edge of the gardens. Bridgeman had enclosed a large part of the gardens within a ha-ha wall – a wall having the *effect* of a terrace or viewing-platform looking out over the country-side, but made by digging a ditch on the outer side, rather than by raising a terrace (see Chapter Three) – and this wall was given rounded bastions at several of the angles or corners round the gardens.

FORMALITY AND NATURALNESS

The last great formal gardens in this country in
the French tradition are St Paul's Walden Bury
and Bicton. At St Paul's Walden Bury, the
house and gardens were begun around 1730 for
Edward Gilbert. The garden designer is still
unknown, but in my opinion at least seized the
'capability' of the site with entire success. It is a
rare design, comparable only with Bramham
Park for the genial use of undulating terrain,
over which straight *allées* or walks are cut
through the woodland, achieving a combination of formality (the avenues) and naturalness
(the ups-and-downs of the ground) which is
both unusual and delightful. While at Bramham
the walks are related more to each other and to
the garden monuments than to the house, the
design at St Paul's Walden Bury is discreetly, yet
firmly linked to the house. Northwards from
the house, a lawn opens on to three axial
avenues or rides, the side and central lines of a
diamond- or kite-shaped plan, extending north-
ward through Walk Wood for over half a mile.
This scheme of avenues was originally flanked
with hornbeam hedges (as were those at Versailles), and is aligned on monuments within or
outside the gardens – statues of Hercules or
Diana, or the church in St Paul's Walden. (The
hornbeam hedges of this design were replaced
by beech in the 1930s, at a time when much
modern garden development was undertaken.)
One happy area within the woodland is the
Theatre of the Running Footman, where a
terraced clearing with a temple at the upper end,
central lawn and lower pool, provides a perfect
parallel to the Italian idea of the *giardino
segreto*.

Bicton's eighteenth-century garden has none
of the subtlety of St Paul's Walden Bury, but the
serene confidence of a sloping, axial layout in
the finest Le Nôtre manner. As at Melbourne,
terraces slope down towards a rectangular pool
with a central fountain. This layout dates from
about 1735, and in 1743 the Obelisk was raised
on the rising ground beyond to complete the
vista. Round three sides of the fountain pond
are narrow flanking canals. This garden was
laid out for Henry Rolle (later Lord Rolle of
Stevenstone) and is still attributed by some to
a design by Le Nôtre. It is fitting that the
last formal garden in the seventeenth-century
tradition should be as keenly linked with Versailles as were St James's Park or Greenwich in
the time of Charles II.

CASTLE HOWARD

• • •

*I*t is easy to be convinced that the horizon-wide landscapes which surround Castle Howard are a single creation, achieved in the time of Charles Howard, 3rd Earl of Carlisle. He and his architects (and garden experts) – Vanbrugh, London, Hawksmoor were the principal figures – did indeed conceive and execute the 'sublime' landscape which Walpole and a host of other admirers praised so highly. Yet the Castle Howard which we see today has undergone many stages of development, both during the 3rd Earl's time, and afterwards.

Of these changes, none is more interesting than the history of the south parterre. Today, enclosed by yew hedges, the lawns and Atlas Fountain are a composite 1850s–1890s creation, gently modified in the following hundred years. Going backwards, there was a parterre design of dazzling intricacy (by Nesfield) in the 1850s; before, in the later eighteenth century, a period of somewhat untidy neglect; and, in the beginning, around 1710, Vanbrugh had designed a scheme of gigantic proportions involving huge geometrically cut hedges, obelisks and archways. Argument still continues about the extent to which this first design was ever realized.

Other much-changed areas include Ray Wood, east of the house, with a modern collection of rhododendrons, and the walled kitchen gardens, begun by Vanbrugh around 1703, and now containing one of the most comprehensive collections of old roses in the country.

Left: The Atlas Fountain was made the centrepiece of W.A. Nesfield's ornate parterre design at Castle Howard in the 1850s. The present pattern of lawns and yew hedges dates from the 1890s, and was devised by the 9th Countess of Carlisle.

Far left: Vanbrugh's Temple of the Four Winds. From this raised 'bastion' the view embraces the Mausoleum, the New River (or Roman) bridge, and the Pyramid. The Temple is reached along the gently winding terrace walk which was originally the main street of the old village of Henderskelf, moved when the gardens were made.

• • •

'AN AGREEABLE MIXTURE OF GARDEN AND FOREST'

In different ways, the garden and parkland creations of Castle Howard, Cirencester and Studley Royal fall between the formal tradition of the late seventeenth century and the later development of landscape gardening. The house at Castle Howard was built by Vanbrugh for Charles Howard, 3rd Earl of Carlisle, between 1700 and 1721, and Vanbrugh was also deeply involved in the elaboration of the 'sublime' garden scheme. This was however firmly overseen by Lord Carlisle himself, who is thought to have begun garden plans by around 1698, and who continued development of the 'immense project' – affecting some 5000 acres – until his death in 1738 (Vanbrugh had died in 1726). An early plan by George London for formal treatment of Ray or Wray Wood, east of the house, seems to have been executed only in part or much modified by Lord Carlisle (possibly helped, and considerably so, by Stephen Switzer). By 1718, in his *Ichnographia Rustica*, Switzer wrote that he thought 'this incomparable Wood the highest pitch that Natural and Polite Gardening can possibly ever arrive to', though, alas!, we can no longer see the winding paths which led through the woodland to the different clearings, round garden buildings with fountains and cascades.

This gently 'natural' woodland scheme must, in the early years of the eighteenth century, have seemed no less than daring beside the sternly geometrical parterre designed by Vanbrugh, of which the main part was laid out to the south of the house. The grand approach roads – one runs north–south half a mile to the west of the house, and the other east–west to arrive on the north side of the house – were equally uncompromising in their geometry. But the long north–south road, dead straight for three miles, is disturbingly unclassical in its architecture. Two gates – the Carrmire Gate by Hawksmoor (after 1726), and the Pyramid Gate by Vanbrugh (1719) with flanking walls of about 1720–5, and wings added in 1756 – give a profoundly English and would-be feudal air to the approach, with their battlements, towers and turrets suggesting that the visitor is within the ancient confines of a heavily fortified castle.

Closer to the house – to Castle Howard – the axis eastwards from the south front leads to the curving terrace walk, flanked on one side by statues, which opens on to the raised, grassy

bastion (effectively a ha-ha wall) on which stands the Temple of the Four Winds. Designed by Vanbrugh, built after his death, this must be one of the supreme garden buildings, both for its *design* – Palladian, referring like the villa at Chiswick to the Villa Capra – and for its *site* – overlooking, to east, south and west, a prospect extending for several miles over field and valley, woodland and moor. Further to the south-east is Hawksmoor's Mausoleum, designed 1728–9, and southwards is the New River (or Roman) Bridge (*c.* 1740) by Daniel Garrett. On the skyline, round to the south-west, is the Pyramid (by Hawksmoor, also 1728–9). The prospect is immense, unmatched in other English landscape gardens. Walpole's words, written to George Selwyn on 12 August 1772, and often repeated, must be quoted again:

> Nobody had told me that I should at one view see a palace, a town, a fortified city, temples on high places, woods worthy of being each a metropolis of the Druids, the noblest lawn in the world fenced by half the horizon, and a mausoleum that would tempt me to be buried alive; in short I have seen gigantic places before but never a sublime one.

Between 1714 and 1718, Allen, 1st Earl Bathurst (1684–1775), had Oakley Lodge drastically remodelled to make Cirencester House, and in 1714 or 1715 began the development of the woodland on the western side of the house – a process which was to continue until his death. In 1716 he added the manor of Sapperton to his property, giving the park a total area of some 2500 acres.

The park at Cirencester is, I imagine, the nearest we have in England to compare with the large landscaped forest areas of Fontainebleau or Compiègne in France – a type of gardening praised by Addison in the *Spectator* (25 June 1712) for its 'artificial Rudeness', 'where we see a large Extent of Ground covered over with an agreeable mixture of Garden and Forest'. Three years later, Switzer's first garden book, *The Nobleman, Gentleman and Gardener's Recreation*, was to praise 'Rural and Extensive Gardening', and 'Extensive or Forest Gardening', and this is indeed what Lord Bathurst undertook at Cirencester. For some thirty years, he was in contact with Alexander Pope about his endeavours. Pope (who had published *Windsor Forest* in 1713) first visited Cirencester in 1718, and thereafter visited house and forest

Above: '*A mausoleum that would tempt me to be buried alive*' *wrote Walpole in 1772. The Mausoleum was designed by Nicholas Hawksmoor in 1728–9, and is an outlying but dominant feature in the eastern landscape at Castle Howard.*

Left: *Lord Bathurst's grand rural avenues at Cirencester are among the last, and the greatest, of England's formal garden schemes. Laid out from 1714 onwards, they may be paralleled by the great avenues at Stansted or Hackwood – or Badminton.*

• • •

Below: The view up the valley from the Moon Ponds at Studley Royal reveals a sublime contrast – the medieval ruins of Fountains Abbey.

• • •

scenes many times until his death in 1744. At first, Pope's letters refer to intentions and young plantations, rather than solid avenues – on 15 September 1721 he wrote to Lady Mary Wortley Montagu of his latest visit, describing 'the future and as yet visionary beauties that are to rise in these scenes', which already inspire him to exclaim that 'no words, nor painting, nor poetry can given the least image proportionate to the daily views of the noble scenes, openings, and avenues of this immense design'.

The principal rides or avenues are the 5-mile-long Broad Avenue, aligned on Cirencester Church, and the mile-long Elm Avenue between the house and the tall column of Queen Anne's Monument (1741). Lesser avenues, such as Windsor Walk, cross the park, and at several of the intersections are monuments – the Hexa-

gon, 1736; Pope's Seat; the Horse Guards. Deep within Oakley Wood is King Alfred's Hall – begun in 1721 and finished in 1732, using old, possibly medieval materials from Sapperton manor house. This building, with pointed windows, round turret and battlements, ranks with the Gothic Pavilion at Shotover (*c.* 1720) as one of the very first 'mock-Gothic' constructions of the eighteenth century. Gardens were to prove a fertile setting for the buildings of the Gothic revival – ending in the 1790s with the greatest of all Gothic follies, William Beckford's gigantic and short-lived Fonthill Abbey, set within a walled and totally private forest paradise.

Roughly contemporary with these still formal schemes is the woodland layout at Hackwood, within the much larger, and medieval, deer park. The alleys and avenues related

to Spring Wood were probably laid out by about 1720. In November 1754, Pococke's travel journal engagingly records that 'the walks, wood, and lawn in the garden are very fine, and it is adorn'd with statues, particularly an equestrian statue of ——'. This memorable, yet unremembered statue is of George I, and must be of similar date to that opposite the north front at Stowe (by John Van Nost, 1723).

Still somewhat formal is the geometrical canal at Frampton Court, overlooked at its northern end by the Gothic Orangery, attributed to William Halfpenny. The Orangery is thought to date from about 1752, but the canal, stretching serenely south-west for 200 yards, is more likely to date from the 1730s, when Richard Clutterbuck had Frampton Court built. His architect was probably John Strahan, much influenced by the work of Vanbrugh. On the further side of the house, to the south-west, there is an octagonal dovecote, built in 1760. East of the house is a broad expanse of open parkland, with views across to a lake on the far side.

The incomparable Moon Ponds of Studley Royal, the most perfectly conceived of all geometrical gardens in this country, are the work of John Aislabie (1670–1742), who had withdrawn to his Yorkshire property in the early 1720s, following his disgrace and brief imprisonment in the Tower in 1721. He had been Chancellor of the Exchequer from 1714 to 1718, and was implicated in the collapse of the South Sea Bubble in 1720–1. Before this, he had lived mainly at Hall Barn, in Buckinghamshire, where he had gardened for several years.

His garden architect at Hall Barn had been Colen Campbell, who came north with him to design several of the buildings at Studley Royal – the Fishing Lodges, the Banqueting House, the Rotunda and the Octagon Tower. But these buildings are of slight importance beside the serene perfection of the Moon Ponds, designed, so far as we know, by Aislabie himself in the mid-1720s. Here a circular pool, flanked by two crescent pools, is set in smooth lawn, backed by a steeply rising semi-circle of woodland, and enclosed on the other side by the long 'canal' of the river Skell, to which Aislabie had given regular shape around 1718. The Temple of Piety was begun about 1740 and completed by John Aislabie's son William in 1748.

John Aislabie had intended to extend his garden property to include a feature far different in character from this green yet formal semi-

circle of trees and lawn and pools – the gaunt, intricate and historic ruins of Fountains Abbey, half a mile further up the valley of the Skell. The idea, to us, is 'reasonable' – to achieve a contrast of order and wildness, of Classic symmetry and the Gothic sublime; but we look back over two centuries of such contrast, and for Aislabie in the 1720s to dream of this combination was as daring as Vanbrugh's earlier proposal to keep the ruins of Old Woodstock Manor as part of the grandiose scheme of Blenheim. Vanbrugh's suggestion was rejected, and John Aislabie died before his project could be realized.

There is a fascinating parallel at Duncombe nearby, where a formal scheme of lawns, avenues and terraces had been laid out from about 1713 onwards. The owner, Thomas Duncombe, had planned to drive a terrace-walk westwards to overlook the ruins of Rievaulx Abbey – but he died, around 1725, before this could be done. The fulfilment of his scheme, as of John Aislabie's, belongs to a later part of this history.

Above: John Aislabie retired to his Yorkshire property of Studley Royal after political disgrace. By 1718, he had already 'straightened' the river Skell as it passed through this part of the grounds, and the Moon Ponds – a circular pool, flanked by two crescent pools – were added in the mid-1720s.

• • •

Chapter Three

PARADISE REGAINED

• • •

*T*he formal gardens of the seventeenth century were framed by a philosophic and aesthetic idea of the natural world, which said (in simplest and most general terms) that man's duty was to bring back to order all the lands which had lain in barbaric confusion and ugliness since both the (religious) Fall of Man, and the (political and administrative) Fall of the Roman Empire. In such a view, 'nature' – the physical world of trees and plants, rocks and water – was essentially unruly and hostile, however attractive or useful individual elements – flowers or fruits – might be.

By the later seventeenth century, this attitude had been challenged from several points, particularly by philosophers such as Newton and Leibniz, indicating the mathematical perfection of the laws governing the physical universe. On the grandest scale, these laws implied that God, the Creator of all things, had made a world which was physically perfect; at a far lower level, they implied that everything within the natural world was part of his creation, and that therefore 'nature' – the countryside around us – had in itself an element which was divine.

While the Earl of Shaftesbury wrote about this in philosophic terms – in *The Moralists* of 1709 he declared, of nature's extreme forms, 'the wildness pleases' – Joseph Addison wrote to a wider public in the *Spectator* (23 August 1711) that

> The Spacious Firmament on high,
> With all the blue Etherial sky,
> And spangled Heav'ns, a Shining Frame,
> Their great Original proclaim.

Built by Henry Flitcroft in 1754–6, the Pantheon beside the lake at Stourhead presides over Henry Hoare's original arcadian landscape.

• • •

51

. . .

In this period, Addison had written directly of garden matters in the *Tatler* and the *Spectator*, and informed by this philosophical view. While the clipping of trees and bushes (topiary) was 'unnatural', as were the complex patterns of *parterres de broderie*, the forms of rural nature were admirable, where trees still displayed their 'Luxuriancy and Diffusion of Boughs and Branches' (*Spectator*, 25 June 1712). He describes his own (imaginary) garden with its 'Confusion of Kitchin and Parterre, Orchard and Flower Garden' (6 September 1712), and suggests that the outer parts of one's property (the rural, rather than the garden areas) might, with some small 'Additions of Art . . . be thrown into a kind of Garden'. The countryside, therefore, is to be brought into the visual embrace of the garden – and in the process, the estate as a whole may come to resemble a painting: 'a Man might make a pretty Landskip of his own Possessions' (25 June 1712).

A year later Alexander Pope joined in the attack on topiary, with his essay in the *Guardian* (29 September 1713), where he lists a nurseryman's sale list, a 'Catalogue of Greens' offering slightly damaged items of topiary at knockdown prices. The list begins

> Adam and Eve in Yew; Adam, a little shattered by the fall of the Tree of Knowledge in the great storm; Eve and the Serpent very flourishing.
> Noah's ark in Holly, the ribs a little damaged for want of water.
> The Tower of Babel, not yet finished.

In the same year his pastoral poem 'Windsor Forest' describes (among other things) the nobility and naturalness of aged forest trees:

> Here waving groves a chequer'd scene display,
> And part admit, & part exclude the day.

Pope was to advise his friends and patrons on the new, 'natural' style of gardening (Lord Bathurst at Cirencester, Ralph Allen at Prior Park), and from 1719, when he moved to Twickenham, he was to garden keenly himself, developing his five-acre grounds near the Thames, and the grotto-tunnel excavated in about 1722 to connect the grounds with his house. While his gardens have gone, and the grotto is now barely more than a corridor under the road, his influence on garden thought in England until the 1750s was immense. In 1731, his *Epistle to Lord Burlington* was published, in

which Pope may be said to have codified the attitudes to gardening developed in the previous twenty years. Mocking the tasteless, symmetrical and artificial garden displays of 'Timon's Villa', enclosed by a wall on all sides, Pope urges Lord Burlington and the reader to remember *Nature* throughout their garden-work:

> In all, let *Nature* never be forgot.
> Consult the *Genius* of the *Place* in all,
> That tells the Waters or to rise, or fall,
> Or helps th' ambitious Hill the Heav'ns to scale,
> Or scoops in circling Theatres the Vale,

Calls in the Country, catches opening
   Glades,
Joins willing Woods, and varies Shades
   from Shades,
Now breaks, or now directs, th' intending
   Lines,
Paints as you plant, and as you work,
   Designs.

Much ink has been splashed and splattered in
commentary on these lines, and I am sure that
more will flow. We should note particularly that
the characteristics of the *site* itself are to be
considered (rather than the ambitions of the

owner, or the demands made by his house), and
that these will be related to the countryside
around. A garden which 'calls in the Country'
goes back clearly to Addison's ideas in 1712 that
a man 'might make a pretty Landskip of his own
Possessions'. Nature is seen as the *painter*
(forming the 'Landskip') and *designer*, while
man, who plants and works, is merely the agent
of Nature's grand scheme.

By 1731, the date of this poem, it had become
a relatively simple matter to 'call in the country'
to one's garden – something which was not
possible at the beginning of the century. Until
the early eighteenth century, gardens were, of

Right: The ha-ha wall at Rousham, allowing an unimpeded view from the garden out to the countryside. These 'broad and deep ditches', wrote Count Kielmansegge in 1761, 'cannot be noticed or seen until you come close upon them; from the exclamation uttered when this unexpected obstruction was met with, the name ha-ha has originated.'

. . .

necessity, enclosed with visible barriers – walls, hedges, railings and gates – to prevent deer or cattle from entering the garden area. While Tijou's magnificent gates and screens at Hampton Court allowed those within the garden to look through at the park, they remained a *barrier* between the garden and nature. In 1709, the solution was discovered – or at least mentioned, for the first time: the ha-ha wall.

HA! HA'S!

In *La Théorie et la pratique du jardinage* by A.J. Dézallier d'Argenville the device is referred to as follows (I quote from John James' translation of 1712, *The Theory and Practice of Gardening*):

> At present we frequently make Thorough-Views, call'd *Ah, Ah* . . . This Sort of Opening is, on some Occasions, to be preferred, for that it does not shut up the Prospect, as the Bars of a Grill do.

The ha-ha, as it has been called since this time, is a ditch, sunk in the ground along the outer edge of one's garden, and of a depth and breadth big enough to stop animals clambering in. Normally the garden side of the ditch is vertical, faced with brick or stone, while the outer (or 'country') side of the ditch slopes up gently to the normal level of the ground. In this way the ditch is, more or less, unnoticeable from a distance, while the view of the countryside beyond is free and unhindered. Horace Walpole claimed – and I think rightly – that the invention of the ha-ha was the essential prerequisite to the creation of 'landscape gardens'. He wrote (in his *Essay on Modern Gardening*, 1771)

> The capital stroke, the leading step to all that has followed, was . . . the destruction of walls for boundaries, and the invention of fossés [ditches] – an attempt then deemed so astonishing that the common people called them Ha! Ha's! to express their surprise at finding a sudden and unperceived check to their walk.

These 'sudden and unperceived' checks to one's walk were quickly and eagerly added to gardens all over England, allowing a free view out to the country. Walpole suggested that Bridgeman may have been the first to employ the ha-ha in his designs – certainly the extended series of ha-ha walls at Stowe is attributed to him, and it may be that the earliest known ha-

ha, at Blenheim (it is mentioned by the antiquary William Stukeley in 1712), could have influenced him, while he worked there with Henry Wise.

We must not think that these attacks on 'artifice', these exhortations to follow 'nature' in the early eighteenth century led to instant creation of garden jungle. Most often, the developments were tentative, and partial, and undertaken to provide a contrast to the formal elements in the garden, rather than their replacement. To us, looking back past the aggressively 'wild' gardens of Hawkstone, Hackfall or Belsay, the early landscape developments at Chiswick, Claremont or Stowe seem still uncertain, and often (to us) disturbingly punctuated with architectural and sculptural features. Yet to the minds of their creators between 1720 and 1730, the changes were real and considerable, and marked a decisive move away from French-inspired formality to a freer style.

A NEW TASTE IN GARDENING

Though some aspects of the new gardening may be found slightly earlier in other places, Lord Burlington's villa at Chiswick is the clearest starting-point for an account of the English landscape garden. Richard Boyle, 3rd Earl of Burlington, was the most important patron of the arts in Hanoverian England, and himself an architect of talent, adapting the design of his garden-villa at Chiswick (built between about 1723 and 1729) from that of Palladio's Villa Capra (the Villa Rotonda). His interest in Palladian architecture is a part of the renewal of interest in Renaissance and ancient Roman Italy in this period, and for him was coupled with his own experiences of Italy during the Grand Tour. The gardens were first laid out, in the mid-1720s, by Charles Bridgeman, with a

Above: The Ionic temple at Chiswick, exquisite in design and formal setting, is Lord Burlington's own creation, sited here while Bridgeman was laying out the formal features of the gardens in the 1720s. Its perfection of form, with the circular pool and obelisk, bears comparison with Aislabie's Moon Ponds at Studley Royal.

Left: This fine formal garden scheme at Chiswick, beside the conservatory or camellia house, is attributed to Joseph Paxton, brought here briefly from Chatsworth by the 6th Duke of Devonshire in the mid-nineteenth century. It has been excellently restored in the 1980s and presents a varied display of massed bedding in the summer months.

• • •

formal avenue and *patte d'oie* (or 'goose-foot') of radiating paths between clipped hedges, leading to small architectural features – a temple, a column and a bridge. Burlington himself designed the Ionic Temple, facing a circular pond with central obelisk.

These formal elements were then added to by William Kent (1685–1748) in the later 1720s, and mark his first work as a garden designer. Trained as a painter, he had studied in Italy for several years (partly at Burlington's expense), and had been employed at Chiswick on the interior decoration of the villa. To Bridgeman's part of the gardens Kent added the lawn,

terminated by clipped hedge-alcoves (the *exedra*) to receive classical statues, the lake and cascade to westward, and the obelisk on the western boundary. Of these, the lake and cascade are of exceptional importance in European garden history – the lake for its *irregular* shoreline, and the three-arched cascade building for its *ruined* appearance. While artists had often drawn or painted real lakes with natural shorelines, and real ruins of Greek or Roman origin, this appears to be the earliest moment at which such 'natural' or 'ancient' characteristics should have been deliberately reproduced in a garden.

STOWE

· · ·

A work to wonder at – perhaps a Stow.' Though Pope misspelt the name, his opinion that these were the most important gardens of his age was right. Among the many experiments and adventures in 'landscaping', the slowly evolving gardens of Stowe remain supreme. As Christopher Hussey said, they are 'the outstanding monument of English landscape gardening'.

At Stowe the plan of the gardens, their design and style all developed and changed in the course of a century – as did the house – involving a galaxy of architects and landscape designers. The gardens began in modest and formal style in the late 1680s, matching a fair-sized mansion, and then, from around 1715, the layout was vastly enlarged and adorned with splendid monuments and temples. By the 1720s Stowe might have seemed to be rivalling Versailles.

Yet the designer of the gardens at this point, Charles Bridgeman, was not wholly committed to formal magnificence – he was among the first in England to look (albeit timidly) towards the countryside. He built a ha-ha wall round much of his huge scheme which allowed vistas outwards into the park. In the 1730s Bridgeman was followed by William Kent, who began to 'soften' the earlier rigid outlines of paths and avenues. East of the main axis he created the gentle Elysian Fields, an evocation of the spirit of classical Italy, as seen in the paintings of Claude Lorrain or Gaspard Poussin.

A rougher and more 'natural' landscape was developed in Hawkwell Field. Here Kent may have been helped by the young Lancelot Brown, who was head gardener at Stowe from 1741 until he left, in 1751, to set up his own practice.

Above: *This landscape view from one of the twin Lake Pavilions was developed over some eighty years. Beginning as a rigid formal axis, with clipped avenues, geometrical pools and fountains, its present state was reached in the 1770s after the Octagon Lake had been remodelled as a 'natural' lake.*

Left: *Stowe's Palladian Bridge was built by 1738, in direct imitation of the bridge at Wilton. It carries the circuit drive round the eastern side of the gardens, and up to the 'landscape' of Hawkwell Field.*

Far left: *Kent's design for the Temple of British Worthies was first intended for Lord Burlington's villa at Chiswick. Built at Stowe in about 1735, it enshrines the busts of the great Britons of the past – such as Shakespeare, Queen Elizabeth, Isaac Newton and the Black Prince.*

• • •

Above: The Oxford Bridge (1761) carries the western approach drive to Stowe over an artificial lake, towards the Boycott Pavilions, built around 1728. Similar 'Roman' bridges were sited in many garden landscapes, such as Castle Howard, Stourhead, Chatsworth and Compton Verney.

• • •

Kent's work was quickly appreciated, and he became involved in numerous garden projects. In 1734 he was credited by Sir Thomas Robinson with inventing 'a new taste in gardening'. 'Mr. Kent's notion' was 'to lay them out, and work without either level or line' – i.e. to design his gardens, not as drawing-board exercises, basically geometrical and symmetrical, but as *landscapes*, for which his training as a painter, and his experience in Italy, fitted him admirably.

From Chiswick, Kent moved on to several other gardens where Bridgeman had already worked – particularly to Stowe, Rousham and Claremont. (We might note, however, that in one instance at least, at Houghton Hall, where the main plan for Sir Robert Walpole was worked out between 1720 and 1724, and where Bridgeman or his follower 'Mr. Eyre' were involved around 1725–7, Kent's part seems to have been related solely to architectural matters. The fine Water House, or Water Tower, probably designed by Lord Pembroke and completed in 1732, forms a focal point some 600 yards north of Houghton Hall along one of the main avenues.) At Stowe, in the mid-1730s, Kent's main contribution was in the Elysian Fields, eastwards from the main north–south axis. In this small valley, he designed the Temple of British Worthies on one side of the stream,

the Shell Bridge which crosses it, and the Temple of Ancient Virtue on the other. Not far from the Temple of Ancient Virtue (built in complete form and modelled on the ruined Temple of the Sibyl at Tivoli) Kent had built a Temple of Modern Virtue, in ruins. It has gone. We may wonder again, looking back two centuries, what Kent would think, now that his three-dimensional allegory of modern frailty has disappeared? The overall conception may possibly be attributed to Lord Cobham himself, but Kent's part in the landscaping is also accepted, influenced by his experience of Italian scenery, and his knowledge of paintings of the Italian landscape by Claude Lorrain and Gaspard Poussin. The Elysian Fields represent, as firmly as the lake and cascade at Chiswick, another decisive advance in the idea of the landscape garden – this time, the representation in three dimensions of the idealized landscapes, with classical buildings, shown in these paintings.

By about 1739 a further development east of the Elysian Fields was begun by Lord Cobham with Kent's guidance: the undulating area of Hawkwell Field. Here the character of the scene is more rural – a broad open pasture, rising at the centre, so that the whole expanse cannot be seen at once, with buildings set far apart, each existing in its own right within the rolling

landscape. To the south is the Temple of Friendship, by James Gibbs, 1739; slightly north is the Palladian Bridge, *c.* 1738, possibly by Gibbs, and hot on the heels of the original version at Wilton. The bridge at Stowe crosses the far eastern arm of the Octagon Pool, vastly changed from its first firm geometry to a loose country-pond outline. At the highest point of Hawkwell Field is Gibbs' Gothic Temple (built by 1744). It was first called the Temple of Saxon Liberty, since the Saxons were then thought to have been free-living citizens – in contrast to the voteless French, subjects of a tyrant-king – and built in a deliberately irregular form (three-sided, and with towers or turrets of varied height) to contrast with the regular buildings of France. At the far, northern end of Hawkwell Field was another classical building, the Lady's Temple, so remote that it did not clash with the rural and Gothic scenes described before.

Kent died in 1748, and it is thought that in his last years, he may have begun the process of 'softening' the rectilinear appearance of Bridgeman's walks and avenues to south and southwest of the house – a process which continued into the mid-1770s, ending with the virtual transformation of these areas from formal to natural landscape, retaining the architectural features without their original connecting paths. The main southern axis was to undergo the most striking change, losing all trace of terraces, clipped flanking hedges and fountains, and being grassed over all the way from the house to the Octagon Lake, which was turned into a 'natural' pond (though still called the Octagon Lake, or Pool). To east and west of this broad and grassy axis, the woodland now rises in belts and clumps of studied irregularity.

Though never owning the galaxy of garden buildings and monuments found at Stowe (over thirty survive today), the gardens of Claremont have a history which embraces as many designers, several of whom were also at Stowe. In 1708 John Vanbrugh designed the first house at Claremont, and some six or seven years later built the Belvedere, a square battlemented tower with turrets which still looms over the woodland, one of the first examples of the 'Gothic revival', and related to his battlemented approach-walls at Castle Howard. From the Belvedere, a grass walk led downhill to the bowling green, and then to the amphitheatre (*c.* 1724), designed by Bridgeman as part of a generally geometrical layout. The amphitheatre – a sloping semi-circle of grassy terraces – overlooks the lake. In Bridgeman's scheme, this lake was circular, but in the early 1730s Kent was called in – as at Chiswick, Stowe and Rousham – and re-shaped it (as he re-shaped the Octagon Lake at Stowe) giving it a natural

Above: The island and its tree-girt temple are a part of William Kent's contribution to the complex landscape at Claremont, around 1738. Before Kent, the gardens had been shaped by Vanbrugh and Bridgeman; after came Brown, and then others . . .

• • •

outline, and including an island, with a temple, constructed in about 1738. Beside the lake, he made a three-arched grotto rather like his cascade at Chiswick. Though this was altered in the mid-eighteenth century, it is recognizably Kentian, and its pattern of careful dilapidation reappears in the same period in the rough, time-worn masonry of the cascade in Venus' Vale, at his surviving masterwork, Rousham.

AN ENGLISH DAPHNE

Bridgeman had laid out gardens at Rousham around 1720, covering an irregular and sloping site between the house and the course of the river Cherwell with several regular features – the bowling green, in front of the house, a 'theatre', two square pools, and the Long Walk. Kent was called in later and by about 1738 was employed by General James Dormer to remodel both the house and the gardens. Some of Bridgeman's features remain – notably the Long Walk and the bowling green – but Kent added others, and gave to the whole (about 25 acres) a singularly Arcadian quality, which made Rousham one of the most complete and beautiful of early landscape gardens – 'Kentissime' as Horace Walpole put it. Within the gardens, Kent devised a series of 'scenes', connected by paths, yet carefully concealed one from another, so that the different buildings or sculptures are revealed to the visitor in a controlled sequence; and, again and again, these scenes incorporate different views *out* over the Oxfordshire countryside. Most of the time, the house is out of sight, and the character of the gardens is influenced by the statuary, and small, mainly classical buildings which one passes, moving from scene to scene, and by the rural vistas which open beyond, across the winding river to the fields. 'The whole [wrote Walpole] is as elegant and antique as if the emperor Julian had selected the most pleasing solitude about Daphne to enjoy a philosophic retirement.' But Daphne was near Antioch, in Syria, and Rousham is in England. Across the river Cherwell, Kent adorned an old mill with flying buttresses, pinnacles and a little belfry, to make it look 'Gothic', and on the skyline, he built the 'Eyecatcher' – a three-arched, battlemented outline which still stands, a gaunt and near-to-prehistoric silhouette.

To finish this series of gardens in which William Kent had an important part, we should refer to the adjacent areas of Kensington Gar-dens and Hyde Park. While they now present features which are mainly of the nineteenth and twentieth centuries, both have long histories – Hyde Park beginning as a deer park in the sixteenth century, and Kensington Gardens being developed a century later, using land taken from Hyde Park for the gardens of Kensington Palace. These gardens, of formal design, partly the work of London and Wise, were re-developed by Stephen Switzer and Charles Bridgeman in the early eighteenth century. Virtually all trace of their work has gone, obliterated first by Kent in the 1730s, and then by more modern developments. Kent's part remains a vital element of the two areas, since he was responsible for damming the little river Westbourne, to create the sinuous lakes named the Long Water and the Serpentine. Already at Chiswick his lake had been called the 'Serpentine River' by Defoe, and at Rousham he made an S-shaped stream called the Serpentine Rill. In the aesthetics of the 1730s and 1740s, the S-shaped line was considered to be the 'line of beauty', the perfect compromise between excessive symmetry and jagged disorder.

GARDEN MANIA

From the 1730s to the mid-eighteenth century, the gardens and grounds at Goodwood were much taken up with the *furor hortensis*, or 'garden mania'. While the designer is not certain, much of the enthusiasm came from Charles Lennox, the 2nd Duke of Richmond (1701–50), and Sarah, 2nd Duchess. The Duke was a dendrophile, and Pococke noted in September 1754 that

> this place is most famous for a great variety of forest trees and shrubs; they have thirty different kinds of oaks, and four hundred different American trees and shrubs.

But he also noted the fine viewing pavilion, on a hill nearby – Carné's Seat, built around 1743 by Roger Morris – and the grotto or shell house to one side, whose walls were lavishly decorated with shells in the 1740s by the Duchess and her daughters. The task took – it is said – seven years, and naval officers serving in shell-rich seas were pressed to bring back sackfuls as friendly tribute. The floor, in contrast, is given a star pattern formed from animals teeth, ground to a level and gleaming surface.

Mr Hamilton And Mr Hoare

'How highly wou'd it repay the gardener to keep a garden chair with a small horse; as it is so profitably and agreeably practised at Mr. Hamilton's at Pains Hill?' complained John Byng in 1781, when visiting the garden of Piercefield, in Wales. Garden-visiting had by then become a fashionable amusement and the extent of many 'landscape' gardens made the use of small carriages – such as a low, open 'sociable' – desirable. We should note that these visits were almost always linked with visits to the houses within the gardens, to see the paintings and furniture they held. *There* was the main object, and some of the owners even had accommodation specially built for travellers who had come to see, and admire, their property. This was done by the Earl of Carlisle at Castle Howard, beside the Pyramid Gate, and by Henry Hoare at Stourhead, who built the present inn in Stourton for the purpose.

Left: London's great parks are famous for their avenues. This avenue of plane trees in Kensington Gardens is aligned on the Albert Memorial. Northwards it leads to G.F. Watts' Statue of Physical Energy, erected in 1907.

Below: 'From a belvedere, about half a mile from the house, a very extensive prospect is obtained.' Carné's Seat, in Goodwood Park, was built by Roger Morris around 1743, while the entrancing shell house nearby was being decorated by the Duchess of Kingston and her daughters.

• • •

ROUSHAM

• • •

*H*orace Walpole said that at Rousham, William Kent had created his best landscape garden. Here he was 'Kentissime'. Kent worked at Rousham from the late 1730s, after a partly formal layout had been established by Charles Bridgeman in the 1720s. Happily, Kent's work has survived with little serious change. We may see a daring combination of 'Arcadian' or 'Classical' scenes (incorporating sculpture or monuments which suggest to the visitor 'This is an antique land') and spacious vistas out to the English countryside.

The gardens are laid out along a sloping terrain, bounded by the curving course of the river Cherwell. The river plays a vital part in the scheme, since it does away with the need for any other boundary on this side – no fence, wall, not even a ha-ha – and allows a free prospect out to the Oxfordshire fields beyond. As well as this, its course is emphatically 'natural'; it curves, it *meanders*, and in so doing it varies the outward views, with a subtlety which the straight canals of formal French gardens could never do.

Eastwards from the house is an area which both Bridgeman and Kent left alone – the three older enclosures of the walled kitchen gardens. These are of seventeenth-century origin, and the southern area contains a fine seventeenth-century dovecot. Beyond, to the east, is St James's church. These areas have been used for the last century both for kitchen produce (they retain rows of ancient espaliered apples and a fine area of soft fruit), and for flowers. The northern garden has a good double herbaceous border, the southern has a recently developed rose garden, the roses contained within neat box hedges.

Above right: In one of the walled gardens to the east of the house, stands the fine dovecot, dated 1685.

Right: 'Praeneste', the arcaded terrace and viewing-point, looks east across to the water meadows beyond the Cherwell. This garden building, designed by William Kent, still contains Kent's elegant wooden benches.

Far right: In Venus' Vale, this pool is fed both from a small cascade, and from the 'Serpentine rill', and itself feeds a larger three-arched cascade below.

• • •

At 'Mr. Hamilton's at Pains Hill' however, it was above all the gardens people came to see – his house was small, and not noted for elegance. Charles Hamilton acquired 125 acres near Cobham in 1738, adding another 75 acres or so soon after. The ground had not been gardened before – he began from scratch, and his efforts quickly attracted attention and approval. In 1748, Walpole could write that Hamilton 'has really made a fine place out of a most cursed hill'. By then, Walpole could have seen richly varied plantations of trees and shrubs – including many recently introduced American conifers – grassy paths and entrancing sweeps of lawn, and a winding lake, which was fed with water pumped up from the river Mole. The luxuriant growth and 'natural' planting of the conifers gave a wildness to parts of the gardens which visitors were willing to compare with landscapes of savage, mountainous regions by Salvator Rosa.

Hamilton was an ardent gardener, but he was not rich, and the addition of garden buildings and monuments as solid as those of Castle Howard or Stowe was never in his means. In the mid-1750s he borrowed money in order to build, and by 1758–60, the Painshill landscape

was given a Gothic belvedere, a Turkish tent, bridges, a classical temple, a ruined mausoleum, a Gothic 'tent' or pavilion, a hermitage (briefly housing a hired hermit!) and a grotto. The grotto was enlarged around 1770, when the lake was extended.

In 1771, John Wesley was a visitor to Painshill. The gardens were 'inexpressibly pleasant', he wrote, but added

> And now, after spending his life in bringing it to perfection, the grey-headed owner advertises it to be sold!

Hamilton had overspent. He sold up, and left in 1773. But his reputation as an amateur garden expert could hardly have been higher, and friends consulted him for advice until his death in 1786. One of those with whom his garden contacts lasted for many years was Henry Hoare, of Stourhead (and we should note as well that a part of Hamilton's borrowing had been from Hoare's Bank, in which Henry Hoare was the senior member).

Henry Hoare had inherited the Stourhead estate from his father in 1725, but his garden-making did not begin until 1743 or 44. Like Hamilton, he was an amateur, and likewise began his gardens almost from scratch. But, in contrast, he was wealthy, and throughout his development of the Stourhead site (until about 1783), his schemes were marked by his ability to commission artists and craftsmen on a lavish scale. Henry Flitcroft was his main architect, John Cheere and Michael Rysbrack his sculptors.

As at Painshill, the house at Stourhead is not visible from the gardens. The visit to the gardens is therefore made without the presence of the house forming a part of the experience – a situation vitally different from that in gardens made in the French style, where the house, and the authority it represents, are seen or felt all through the gardens. Here at Stourhead, the gardens, with their central lake and islands, surrounded by richly wooded slopes, adorned with elegant temples and monuments, represent a 'world' which is deliberately separate from that of the grand house and its social connections. As at Rousham, where Kent created visions of a classical and 'philosophic' retirement, Stourhead offers a three-dimensional form of scenes from the antique world. Some – Henry Hoare included – compared views at Stourhead with paintings by Gaspard Poussin or Claude Lorrain; others have suggested links with Virgil's *Aeneid*, and Walpole in his *Essay on Modern Gardening* claimed that Stourhead was closer to Milton's description of paradise than anything Claude had painted.

By about 1755, the lake, with the Temple of Flora, the grotto and the Pantheon, had been completed; by the mid-1760s Hoare added the Roman bridge and the Temple of Apollo, and seems also to have had much contact and discussion with Hamilton to do with later features – the hermitage and a Turkish tent, both of which have gone, and the Convent and Alfred's Tower, buildings erected far off in the western woodland, remote from the main gardens and lake. In 1783, Henry Hoare retired from Stourhead to London, and the estate and gardens were taken over by his grandson, Sir Richard Colt Hoare, whose principal contribution was the introduction of a variety of rare trees and flowering shrubs – notably rhododendron and azalea – which give Stourhead a nineteenth-century brilliance of colour at certain periods of the year.

THE WAVING LINE

William Shenstone (1714–63) inherited The Leasowes, a grazing farm of about 150 acres, in 1735. He lived there until his death, converting the farm – fields, hedgerows, orchard and woodland – into a *ferme ornée* from about 1743. Philip Southcote (1698–1758) at Woburn Farm in Surrey is a contender for the invention of the term, but Shenstone is its most influential

Below: This view over the Priory Pool at The Leasowes is part of the landscape of William Shenstone's 'perfectly Arcadian farm', which he adorned with small monuments and poetic inscriptions.

• • •

exponent. Shenstone's income was only £300 a year, and he could never rebuild his old farmhouse home, nor could he give his property buildings or monuments of other than modest materials and proportions. An amateur, and garden-making at roughly the same time as Hamilton and Henry Hoare, his path does not seem to have crossed with theirs, though they undoubtedly knew of him, and he of them. He was a minor literary figure, publishing poems and essays, and corresponding with a wide circle of artistic and literary friends, more often than not in connection with garden matters, where his advice was regularly required.

The Leasowes was as keenly visited as any garden in the mid-eighteenth century and, though unkinder spirits might laugh at the frailty of his 'Gothic screens', his achievement was immensely respected, and numerous descriptions survive to give both the character and the detail of his creation, 'this perfectly Arcadian farm'. In particular, there is Robert Dodsley's 'Description of The Leasowes', published in 1764, in the second volume of Shenstone's *Works*. The same volume contains Shenstone's own 'Unconnected Thoughts on Gardening', a rambling yet genial collection of

Shenstone's garden wisdom – a text which was to be frequently reprinted, and to influence the next generation of landscape gardeners.

In his day, Shenstone's *ferme ornée*, or 'ornamental farm', was given a long, roughly circular walk, with multiple views across the farm, or out into the country. There were over forty points along the winding walk where one might stop, reflect and savour the scene, with an abundance of poetic indications – ruins, statues, urns, inscriptions in English or Latin – to suggest what feelings were appropriate. At the most beautiful and extensive viewpoint, the inscription read DIVINI GLORIA RURIS – 'The glory of the divine countryside'.

Urns and inscriptions have gone, but the walk remains. The Leasowes is now a golf course, flanked by areas of public park. Its original area has hardly changed.

The owners of Hagley Hall and Farnborough Hall were both acquaintances and neighbours of Shenstone, also amateur gardeners, and living near enough to visit each other. Lord George Lyttleton at Hagley was infinitely the grandest of these landowners, and began to landscape his extensive park and hilly woodland in the late 1740s – before, in fact, his new

Right: 'A ruined castle, built by Miller, that . . . has the true rust of the Baron's Wars.' Sanderson Miller's ruined castle was built on hilly ground in Hagley Park in 1747–8, and is both a landmark in the parkland, and in the progress of the Gothic revival. 'Ruined' buildings soon became commonplace in garden landscapes.

• • •

Left: *The obelisk, dated 1751, stands at the southern end of the sinuous terrace walk at Farnborough Hall. From this walk, created from 1745 onwards, there are magnificent views westwards towards Edge Hill.*

• • •

house was built in 1754–60. In his landscaping, he was advised and helped by other amateurs – a little by Shenstone, and a great deal by Sanderson Miller, architect, antiquarian, and a leading light among enthusiasts for the Gothic. Sanderson was the main designer of Lyttleton's new house, and also – before the house – of the ruined castle, half a mile eastwards from Hagley Hall, which was the first Gothic building to be built in a deliberately ruined state (in 1747–8). Walpole, in September 1753, wrote to Richard Bentley that the house was 'immeasurably bad and old', but that there was 'a ruined castle, built by Miller, that . . . has the true rust of the Barons' Wars.' Years later, in 1781, John Byng visited Hagley. Though the house displeased him, he succinctly praised the castle as 'a well-built and well-understood ruin'.

Walpole was too early to see the Temple of Theseus (by James 'Athenian' Stuart, 1758–9), the earliest example in England of the primitive Doric, and followed soon after by a similar building at Shugborough; but his enthusiasm for Hagley was genuine: 'such lawns, such wood, rills, cascades, and a thickness of verdure quite to the summit of the hill . . . There is extreme taste in the park . . . there is not one absurdity.' Years later, in his *Essay on Modern Gardening*, he was to link Hagley with Stourhead, in comparing them with Milton's description of paradise.

A visitor to The Leasowes in 1756 composed a poem in which the garden's felicitous use of the 'waving' or 'serpentine' line was highly praised:

Yon stream that wanders down the dale,
The spiral wood, the winding vale,
The path, which wrought with hidden skill
Slow twining scales yon distant hill
With fir invested – all combine
To recommend the WAVING LINE.

Not many miles away, in neighbouring Warwickshire, a friend of Shenstone's, William Holbech, had brought in a common acquaintance, Sanderson Miller (the same who had designed the ruined castle at Hagley) to help him landscape his grounds at Farnborough Hall. Between 1745 and 1751, the noble Terrace Walk was laid out, with its Ionic temple, Oval temple and obelisk. The Terrace Walk is in my opinion the most noteworthy example of the serpentine line in garden design. It winds gently southwards from the house for nearly half a mile, following the contour of the ground, and giving the visitor panoramic, and changing, views over the four pools (one with a cascade) in the lower parts of the gardens, and outwards to the west as far as Edge Hill. Above the terrace is a fringe of woodland, and there are 'promontories' or 'bastions' of laurel downhill. In 1767, in his poem *Edge-Hill*, Richard Jago wrote

Where the tall pillar lifts its taper head,
Her spacious terrace and surrounding lawns,
Deck'd with no sparing cost of planted tufts,
Or ornamental building, Farnborough boasts.

 **Right:** *A part of one of the most individual of all landscape gardens – the view at West Wycombe of Revett's Music Temple (1778–80) on the main island in the lake, with St Laurence's Church high up on Church Hill beyond. The golden ball on the tower was added by Sir Francis Dashwood around 1748.*

• • •

PARADISE IN WEST WYCOMBE

Of the gardens and parks created by distinguished amateurs in the eighteenth century, West Wycombe Park is easily the most original. It bears the stamp of Sir Francis Dashwood (1708–81, created Lord Le Despencer in 1763), who was active in the elaboration of the garden scheme from the mid-1730s until his death. Like Henry Hoare at Stourhead, he employed professionals to execute his wishes – architects such as G.N. Servandoni and Nicholas Revett, and Maurice Louis Jolivet for the first stage of the gardens, Thomas Cook for the second – but the conception is clearly his own.

In the mid- or late 1730s Dashwood had the lake created to the north-east of the house. At this period it was shaped like a swan, and nearby, on the Mount, the Temple of Venus was built in 1748. Meanwhile, on the summit of Church Hill (outside the park, but visible as a landscape feature), the tower of St Laurence's Church was given the gilded sphere, large enough to seat thirteen people, and the chalk of the hill itself was excavated between 1748 and 1752 to create a labyrinthine series of tunnels and larger chambers – the Hellfire Caves. In 1759, the Temple of the Winds was built, 350 yards eastwards from the house, a curious and memorable version (the first in England) of its Athenian original.

In 1764–5, Dashwood had the gaunt hexagonal Mausoleum built close to the church – and equally visible as a part of the landscape – and then, in the 1770s, he embarked on further and extensive developments, of which Revett's Music Temple, on an island in the lake, and the remodelled cascade on the east side of the lake, are the most important survivors after thinning and simplifying by Humphry Repton later.

By 1773, Benjamin Franklin – several times a guest of Dashwood – could write: 'the gardens are a paradise'. The house and lake and temples survive in tranquil and inspiring completeness today, encircled by wooded hills, and overlooked, to the north, by the church, golden ball and mausoleum; to the south, by the statue of a Roman horseman, erected in 1986.

Left: The Temple of the Winds in West Wycombe Park, erected in 1759 in imitation of the original in Athens. The rising farmland beyond is separated from the gardens by a long and impressive ha-ha wall, stretching for 500 yards towards the house.

• • •

Chapter Four

ONE BROWN . . .

• • •

*O*n 22 July 1751, Horace Walpole wrote to George Montague of what he had seen at Warwick Castle. The castle itself was 'enchanting', while outside

> The view pleased me more than I can express; the river Avon tumbles down a cascade at the foot of it. It is well laid out by one Brown who has set up on a few ideas of Kent and Mr. Southcote.

As so often, Horrie was quick off the mark. By the mid-century, not a few had 'set up' on the ideas of the new landscape garden, and more were to follow, encouraged in part by the happy, if misleading, notion that if Kent had worked 'without level or line', they might do the same. Not all were unqualified, nor were they incapable. William Eames or Emes, F. (possibly Francis) Richardson, Thomas Greening, Samuel Lapidge, Thomas Sandby, John Spyers, John Webb, Thomas White, Richard Woods are among those whose names appear as professional garden designers in the second half of the century (Lapidge and Spyers are known mostly for their work for Brown, who employed them both as assistants in 1765). Beside these practitioners, there are many private people – owners, or affluent amateur advisers – who took to 'landscaping' their own property, and in so doing often modified, or removed entirely, the gardens of a formal kind which their ancestors had made.

Towering above them is Lancelot Brown (1716–83), known as 'Capability' Brown from

This tranquil lake was created at Bowood in the 1760s for the 2nd Earl of Shelburne. It is one of his purest and most lovely surviving works, little changed since the eighteenth century.

• • •

Below: Capability Brown's lake at Petworth was created in the early 1750s. For two centuries it has looked as if it was always there – yet it is artificial, an idealized form of nature, made by man.

• • •

his habit of referring to the 'capabilities' of the sites on which he was asked to advise. Born in Northumberland, his first garden experience was in northern England, but in 1741 he came to work at Stowe where he stayed for ten years. Kent remained in charge of landscape developments at Stowe until his death in 1748, and Brown had therefore long and fruitful contact with him at this most important of all landscape gardens.

Brown's part in the elaboration of the Stowe landscape is still uncertain, but it is clear that he had begun to work at other gardens some years before he left Stowe in 1751 to set up in independent practice. The gardens and parkland at Warwick Castle were one of his more extensive early projects, lasting from 1749 onwards, and continuing with interruptions until 1761. He began by replacing old formal gardens round the castle with grass and scattered trees, and then, around 1755, developing the parkland south of the river Avon, obliterating most of the earlier straight rides, and adding belts of trees and woodland round the boundaries, to enclose a long carriage drive round the park.

Francis, Lord Brooke, who had called Brown in, is praised by Jago in *Edge-Hill*:

Nor spares his generous mind
The cost of rural work, plantation large,
Forest, or fragrant shrub; or shelter'd walks,
Or ample, verdant lawns, where the sleek deer
Sport on the brink of Avon's flood, or graze
Beneath the rising walls.

Most of Brown's parkland survives, though 'the rising walls' of Warwick Castle now overlook some fine areas of formal gardens, laid out by Robert Marnock in 1868–9.

'AN AMPLE LAKE IN CRYSTAL PEACE'

At Petworth, George London had laid out a formal terrace scheme west of the house, and a wilderness – likewise formal, with clipped hedges – to northwards. Brown was called in in 1751–2, his work continuing until at least 1756. He drastically changed the formal wilderness to

an informal area of shrubs and trees, which included a Doric temple and an Ionic rotunda, while the late seventeenth-century terrace scheme was wholly swept away, replaced by lawns sweeping out from the very front of the house into the park, with the lake, new-created, mid-way in the prospect. In Book III of *The English Garden* (1772), William Mason asked – and then answered – this question:

Is there within the circle of thy view
Some sedgy flat, where the late ripen'd sheaves
Stand brown with unblest mildew? 'tis the bed
On which an ample lake in crystal peace
Might sleep majestic.

This creation of landscape lakes was above all Capability Brown's characteristic and central work. Again and again, he gave to his clients' property the vista, prospect – illusion even – of expansive water, a level, mirror-like surface contrasting with the undulating lawns, the clumps of trees, or the belts of encircling woodland. As at Petworth, where Brown's lake,

park and trees survive in tranquil majesty, most of his lakes were formed by damming a stream, and allowing the water to rise up round the natural contours of the ground. Sometimes, these contours were 'adjusted', to give a more pleasing – or extensive – shoreline, and the lakes might well incorporate earlier pools or fish-ponds. Less often, the estate might already possess a main water feature – such as the river Avon at Warwick Castle – needing little or no elaboration in itself, but which Brown's land-scaping would then reveal, or partly conceal, to best advantage.

The lake at Croome Court is a typical Brown creation, formed from stream water (the Bourne Brook) and from drainage culverts from the vicinity of the house. The lake – a long and sinuous 'river', with two islands at the northern end, a weir to the south – served therefore both the landscape purpose, and the necessary drainage of the area of the founda-tions. Brown, who was first called in around 1750, worked intermittently at Croome Court until the 1770s, collaborating first with San-derson Miller (both in designing a new house for

Below: Beyond the lake at Petworth, Brown's parkland extends to the horizon. Like the lake, it looks entirely nature's creation.

. . .

. . .

the Earl of Coventry, and in the scheme for the park) and later with Robert Adam. Miller, Brown and Adam are variously credited with buildings in the park and grounds – the Gothic Dunstall Castle (Miller), a Corinthian summer-house on the main island, a grotto, a rotunda, and the church of St Mary Magdalene (Brown), and the circular Panorama Tower a mile west of the house (Adam). Adam decorated the interior of the church, and further garden buildings including a Gothic ruin were added by James Wyatt between 1794 and 1801. One of Brown's most complex schemes, the house and park-land at Croome Court are now in divided ownership.

Brown's work at Bowood survives in singular beauty and purity. His main work, for the 2nd Earl of Shelburne, was between 1763 and 1766,

but he had been consulted as early as 1757 by the 1st Earl. By damming the waters of two streams, the Washway and the Whetham Brook, he created a winding lake one and a half miles long. The dam is at the northern end. In about 1785, the overflow from the dam was made much more picturesque, being given a cascade, de-signed by Charles Hamilton (of Painshill), and grotto-work by Josiah Lane.

Unlike Croome Court, which had numerous garden buildings, the landscape at Bowood is far less dependent on these, having, in Brown's day, only the house itself, west of the lake, and Adam's Mausoleum (1761) to the south-west as architectural features. A small Doric temple was erected in 1864 on a promontory on the eastern side.

At Bowood, as in so many of Brown's gardens, interest and attention are held, not by the multiplicity of monuments in the landscape, but by the landscape itself – the presentation of idealized countryside, 'lake and lawn and trees'. In October 1776, Arthur Young wrote that 'Bowood will afford considerable amusement' for 'the water scenes . . . the accompaniment of hanging woods, varied groves, and cultivated slopes . . . Some scenes are truly Elysian'. We might note tht the 'varied groves' were in response to the 2nd Earl's interest in 'curious trees', and that this enthusiasm for rare and interesting shrubs and trees has since been pursued at Bowood for many generations. In the early and mid-nineteenth century, small but fine formal terraced gardens were built south of the stable courts, overlooking the south-eastern view of the lake.

THE LANDSCAPER AT WORK

In contrast to Bowood, the great landscape at Harewood, where Brown was consulted or employed between 1758 and 1781, was devel-oped in several stages. The landscaping of the park, in the mid- and later eighteenth century, was largely Brown's work – to him is attributed the lake, set in the deep valley of the Gawthorp Beck – though other designers were involved, mainly before Brown, and Humphry Repton and J.C. Loudon were both consulted in the early 1800s. In Brown's period, John Carr and Robert Adam were active in building a new house for Edwin Lascelles, and in the 1840s Charles Barry added the imposing formal ter-race gardens on the park side of the house, given elaborate parterres which were restored as

recently as 1983. The depth of the valley is made more striking by dense planting in the outer and higher regions of the park – a procedure adopted by Brown at several other sites, most spectacularly at Chatsworth.

At Wrest Park, where Brown worked in 1758–60, and again in 1769 and 1771, the imposing axis between the house and Archer's pavilion still maintains the formal outline devised in the 1690s. Brown's part in the gardens was confined to 'naturalizing' the stream and ponds which embraced the woodland of the southern area, turning the water into a broad and convincing 'river'. He may also have had a hand in designing the garden bath house – or 'cold plunge' – west of the walled kitchen garden. A monument to Brown was put up in the woodland after 1760, acknowledging his 'professional assistance'.

In contrast with his restraint at Wrest, Brown upset – or swept away – all the old formal gardens at Longleat between 1757 and the early 1760s. In November 1760 Mrs Delany wrote

The gardens are no more. They are succeeded by a fine lawn, a serpentine river, wooded hills, gravel paths meandering round a shrubbery, all modernised by the ingenious and much sought-after Mr. Brown.

The 'serpentine river' was in fact a string of small, narrow lakes, which were somewhat modified by Repton, called in in 1803. In the early nineteenth century, Repton, together with Sir Jeffry Wyatville, made several changes to the gardens, adding new stables, an orangery, and a boathouse and Palladian bridge, though the main lines of Brown's parkland scheme still survive. Mid-nineteenth-century massed bedding schemes were laid out between the house and the orangery, much simplified, and modified, by Russell Page in the 1940s.

Above: The Banqueting House, or Pavilion, at Wrest Park was designed by Thomas Archer and built in 1709–11. Brown's later landscaping did not affect the main garden axis to Archer's Pavilion. Archer also designed the Cascade House at Chatsworth in 1703.

• • •

ALNWICK

$\cdot\;\cdot\;\cdot$

*B*rown's work at Alnwick in the 1770s runs roughly parallel with his landscaping of Syon Park, both properties of the 1st Duke of Northumberland. At Alnwick, the feeling was already strongly medieval and Gothic. Not only was the castle itself an astonishing instance of medieval fortified architecture, rich indeed in English and Scottish history – but the vast estate (largely beside the course of the river Aln) enclosed other medieval remains, such as the fourteenth-century Abbey, Hulne Priory, founded *c*.1240, and the remains of St Leonard's Hospital.

This Gothic tone was elaborated by the architects Paine and Adam in the mid-eighteenth century, working both on the castle (it was further remodelled by Salvin in 1854–6) and on buildings in the park. With the widening of the river Aln by Brown, bridges were added, and a terrace walk was created below the castle. As at Stourhead, with the erection of the Bristol High Cross in 1765, a medieval monument, the Malcolm Cross, was set up in one of the plantations in 1774.

In 1781, Adam added Brizlee Tower, eminently Gothic in its detail, itself a landmark within the park, and (as Aaron Watson wrote in 1891) having outstanding views, of

> Holy Island, and Bamborough, and
> Dunstanburgh, and Warkworth, and
> the wide sea, with the Cheviots lying
> westward, and Flodden Field, and all
> the famous land of Border song and
> story.

Far left: Development of the landscape at Alnwick by no means came to an end after Brown's work in the 1770s. This handsome iron bridge over the Aln is dated 1812.

Left: The prospects at Alnwick are comparable in their heroic scale with those of Castle Howard, though Alnwick Castle gives to the landscape a medieval rather than a Roman feeling.

Below: Brizlee Tower is the work of Robert Adam and it follows a series of such belvederes in landscape gardens, like the Gothic Tower at Painshill and Alfred's Tower at Stourhead.

*Right: James Paine's
bridge, erected in about
1763, crosses the river
Derwent at Chatsworth
in parkland 'landscaped'
by Capability Brown.
The woodland on the
encircling horizon was
also first planted by
Brown in the late 1750s.*

· · ·

DUCAL COMMISSIONS

Most probably in 1760, Brown was called in by
the 1st Duke of Northumberland to advise on
the landscaping of two different and widely
separated properties – Syon Park in Middlesex,
and Alnwick in Northumberland. Brown's
work – at Syon principally from 1767 to 1773, at
Alnwick until at least 1778 – ran parallel to
architectural developments by Robert Adam at
Syon, 1762–9, and by James Paine and Robert
Adam at Alnwick until 1768.

The size and nature of the two estates differ
considerably. Syon, beside the Thames, is a
largely level 200 acres, while Alnwick, spread
over some 2500 acres, is hilly, and crossed by the
valley of the river Aln. None the less, Brown was
to proceed in the same way at each, by enlarging
the water features, by opening out broad views
from the house (or castle), and by planting trees
in blocks or groups nearer to the boundaries of
the estates. At Syon, he obliterated the terraces
built in the sixteenth and seventeenth centuries
and – by means of a ha-ha – gave the house a
broad view eastwards, and views westwards to
the 'serpentine river'. In fact he made two lakes,
on the line of the 'Duke of Northumberland's
River'. By 1761, Dodsley could describe 'a fine
lawn extending from Isleworth to Brentford'
and views across the river 'to the King's gardens
at Richmond as well as up and down the
Thames'. Woodland and a botanical garden
were added round the northern lake. Brown's
lakes and the outer parts of his landscape
remain, enclosing the notable garden developments undertaken in the nineteenth century by
the 3rd Duke.

At Alnwick, there were no large, earlier
garden works for Brown to clear away. As late
as the mid-century, Canaletto had painted the
castle standing on rugged, rocky ground, and
Brown had this area smoothed and grassed
over, and made a terrace walk below the castle.
The winding river Aln was widened by means of
weirs, a cascade was formed, and two bridges,
probably both by Adam, carry the approach
road across the stream. Brown's plantings were
on a heroic scale, clothing the previously bare
hillsides, and Adam's buildings (in some of
which Brown was involved) complement older
structures. High on one slope is Adam's Brizlee
Tower (1781). The remains of the fourteenth-
century abbey are across the river, and in the
separate area of Hulne Park stand the remains
of Hulne Priory, begun *c.* 1240, and given a

summerhouse by Adam (possibly with Brown)
in 1776–8.

In August 1760, Horace Walpole wrote that
at Chatsworth, the 4th Duke of Devonshire was

> making vast plantations, widening and
> raising the River, and carrying the park on
> to the side of it, and levelling a great deal
> of ground to show the River, under the
> direction of Brown.

In September 1768, Walpole was at Chatsworth
again, adding that

> it is much improved . . . many foolish
> waterworks being taken away, oaks and
> rocks taken into the garden, and a magni-
> ficent bridge built.

Brown's work at Chatsworth probably began

in 1760 or a little before, with the removal of most of the formal layout, and the development of the park. Happily, we may think, Grillet's cascade, and Archer's pavilion at its head, were allowed to stay. Though Walpole rejoices at the removal of 'many foolish waterworks', not a few were still there in June 1789, and deplored by John Byng, who found Chatsworth not to his taste. The cascade, when dry, was a 'disagreeable sight', and 'not much better, when cover'd with the dirty water they lower from the hill', while the sprinklings of the 'leaden tree' were 'worthy only of a tea garden in London'. Byng seems to have been blind to Brown's achievement in the park, where he had sensibly widened the river Derwent, by means of a dam (James Paine had designed the fine bridge around 1763 for Brown's new approach drive), and, above

all, planted woodland thickly along the skyline and upper slopes of the valley. Defoe's impression of a 'houling wilderness' could no longer be maintained, with this green and luxuriant fringe heightening the Chatsworth skyline – even if Pastor Moritz, in 1782, might be told that Chatsworth lay 'at the foot of a mountain, whose summit is covered with eternal snow'!

A 'FREER' LOOK

In 1761 Brown began work at Castle Ashby, his activity continuing until at least 1766. As often elsewhere, he was faced with older schemes – at Castle Ashby, a medieval park, given four long, straight avenues in the seventeenth century. Of these, Brown left only the southern avenue intact, abolishing the others, or leaving sections

Below: The vast park and woodland at Holkham were progressively 'landscaped' from the mid-1720s onwards. The present lake – some three-quarters of a mile in length – was altered and extended by Brown, then by Emes, and again by John Webb, between 1762 and 1803.

• • •

as 'clumps', and planting more loosely contoured areas of trees out in the park. A chain of earlier pools was enlarged to make two lakes, Park Pond and Menagerie Pond. By the latter, he built the Ionic temple, backed by a menagerie, and a dairy with classical façade was built nearer to the house. Brown's parkland survives, now overlooked by the great terraced gardens built beside the house in 1865.

The vast parkland at Holkham, first tackled by William Kent with the owner Thomas Coke (later Lord Leicester) in the 1720s, was Brown's subject in 1762. Again his work was to give the somewhat stiff landscaping a freer look – in effect, enlarging the lake and softening its outline, and adding boundary belts and plantations round the gentle, central parkland. Brown was to be followed by Emes, or Eames, in 1784, and John Webb in 1801–3, who brought the lake to its present shape and length, almost three-quarters of a mile. From 1849 to 1872, the great formal terraces south and north of Holkham Hall were added, by Nesfield and Burn.

These modifications occur and reoccur throughout the history of gardens so often that we might think *change* was an intrinsic part of

each and every garden scheme. In 1761, the German traveller Count Kielmansegge wrote of Audley End

The grounds are not remarkable, and will be improved by the changes which the owner is now very busy making.

Both the house, built immensely between *c.* 1605 and 1614, and the varied formal gardens which had accompanied it in the following 120 years, were undergoing change or reduction, after extended neglect. In 1703, William and John Blathwayt had remarked firmly that in the gardens 'instead of flowers, pot-herbs, and fruit trees, one sees only thistles, brambles and thorns'. Brown was called in by Sir John Griffin Griffin a year after Kielmansegge's visit to Audley End, and between 1762 and 1767 he abolished virtually all trace of previous formal schemes. Broad lawns were laid out westwards to the river Cam; the river itself was widened to form a 'lake', and a bridge of three arches by Robert Adam was built across it for the public road in 1764. Brown added plantations on the rising ground west of the Cam, where the Temple of Victory, by Adam, was built in 1772. A broad arc of ha-ha was added by Brown on

the eastern side of the house, to allow a free view outwards over the parkland, while further monuments were added to east and to north-east in the later 1770s and 1790.

Further landscaping within the grounds at Audley End was continued by Richard Woods in 1780, in the 'Elysian Gardens' beside the river Cam, with Adam's 'Tea House' (or Palladian) bridge added 1782–3. Formality returned to the eastern front of the house in 1832, with the flower garden designed by William Sawrey Gilpin, and this scheme has in turn experienced several changes, and continues to evolve.

Left: Adam's Tea House, or Palladian, Bridge in Audley End's 'Elysian Gardens'.

Below: Brown, who laid out this vista at Audley End in the 1760s, might have wondered mildly about the cricketers, though he would have agreed that his grassy spaces beside the Cam had been well maintained.

BLENHEIM: WATER UNDER THE BRIDGE

> Over one of the small water-courses a stone bridge has been built . . . It is a pity that the bridge . . . is so dreadfully out of proportion with the little stream.

This was Count Kielmansegge's comment at Blenheim in 1761. The 4th Duke of Marlborough had inherited the title in 1758, when he was nineteen, and in 1763 he summoned Brown to advise on the landscaping of London and Wise's formal gardens. Vanbrugh's bridge, 'that damn'd bridge', 'without a river', must have been central in the Duke's, and Brown's, concern.

Brown's labours at Blenheim lasted from 1764 to 1774, by which time all that remained of the huge, original formal scheme was Vanbrugh's walled kitchen garden, London's three-mile avenue northwards from the palace, and – of course – Vanbrugh's bridge. To the south of the palace, all trace of the bastioned formal parterre had gone, replaced by sweeping lawns, and to the north, the bridge had been given, to either side, an expanse of water, a lake, an inland sea of such magnitude and natural splendour that it seemed, and has seemed ever since, as if the bridge was necessarily and reasonably crossing the water at the only possible and proper place.

Like everything in gardening, as distinct from nature, the lake is artificial. Its 'naturalness' is achieved by *art* – Brown's genius, in re-grading the slopes of the surrounding parkland – and by *artifice* – Brown's skill in hiding the *end* of the lake, the dam (or 'bottleneck') holding in the waters of the little river Glyme far round the corner to the south-east. This dam is itself made to look 'natural', being constructed as an elaborate rockwork cascade. It is called the Great Cascade, to distinguish it from a lesser dam-cum-cascade further downstream.

George W. Johnson claimed in his *History of English Gardening* (1829) that it was Brown's work at Blenheim which raised him 'to the acme of popularity'. Certainly the lake, 'one of the finest artificial lakes in the world', is Brown's best-known creation. But he was already famous by 1764, being appointed in that year Royal Gardener at Hampton Court and Richmond. Hampton Court he touched but barely (he is credited with planting the Great Vine), and at Richmond (where royal gardens had been made

by Bridgeman, modified by Kent) his work has, like theirs, either been covered over by housing, or obscured by many later developments at Kew, which took over a part of the royal gardens at Richmond. It is probable that his plan for reshaping St James's Park (a royal park) was devised at this time, but his proposals were left for Nash to implement in the 1820s.

LANDSCAPED ENGLAND

In the mid-1760s Brown must have been both famous and frantically busy, visiting the remotest parts of England. He is credited with naturalizing the somewhat rigid lines of the park at Wentworth Castle, in Yorkshire, around 1764, and making the Serpentine River north-east of the great house, which had been enlarged by the 2nd Earl Strafford in the early 1760s. In the same period, 1762–5, he softened the small valley landscape at Prior Park, outside Bath, made for Ralph Allen (with Pope's advice) in the late 1730s. Already in 1756 the Palladian bridge (probably by Richard Jones, and imitating the Palladian bridges at Wilton and Stowe) had been built over a small water feature near the bottom of the valley, and Brown's task, as at Blenheim, was to give an appropriate setting to this magnificent bridge. On sloping ground he created a chain of pools divided by narrow banks, and looking from a distance (from top *or* bottom of the garden) as if they are a single piece of water. Both ends of the chain are concealed by trees, and so, as at Blenheim, the bridge *appears* to be 'naturally' sited, crossing a real waterway.

Bridgeman's formal layout at Wimpole, with its enormous avenue to southwards, had already been 'softened' in the 1750s (though the avenue survives). In 1767–8 Brown was called in, and added characteristic belts of trees along the boundaries. Further changes to the Wimpole landscape were made by Emes in the 1790s, by Repton (Red Book 1801, and further work 1809), and by others in the mid-nineteenth century. He laid out two lakes, with a bridge of seven arches (replaced a century later), and opened up some of the lesser avenues to provide broader views out from the house. The most notable feature of Brown's work today is the vista northwards, which leads to the castellated folly finally put up by Brown in 1772. It had been designed in 1749 by Sanderson Miller (soon after his 'ruined castle' at Hagley), but not built. Brown himself discussed its siting and

Left: This Palladian bridge is the last in the marvellous series of three bridges, begun at Wilton in 1737, followed at Stowe within a year, and completed here at Prior Park in 1756. Brown convincingly reshaped the pools at the bottom of the valley, showing that the bridge really had to be there to cross an important waterway.

Below: At Wimpole, Brown did away with much of Bridgeman's formal layout, and part of Brown's 'natural' landscape was in turn affected by Victorian plantings. But Brown's vista to the north, culminating in the Gothic tower, erected in 1772, remains as a principal feature.

. . .

construction with the owner, the 2nd Earl of Hardwicke, from 1767 onwards.

In the 1760s Robert Adam remodelled and extended the mansion at Compton Verney, and Brown was called in by Lord Willoughby de Broke to landscape the grounds. By 1767, Richard Jago claimed in his poem *Edge-Hill*:

> new culture clothes the scene
> With verdant grass, or variegated grove.
> . . . .
> The glitt'ring stream, with correspondent grace,
> Its course pursues, and o'er th' exulting wave
> The stately bridge a beauteous form displays.

Jago may have been anticipating Brown's achievement, as his landscaping work lasted until 1774. Again, Kent removed small formal gardens near the house, and created one of his nobler lakes, forming the Compton Pools from a string of five much smaller ponds. The serpentine water was crossed by two bridges, one with three arches for the drive to the house, one with five arches for the public road from Warwick to Banbury.

While Brown probably executed both these

Below: Duns Mere and the Rotunda at Highclere. Loudon wrote 'we may venture to call it one of the finest places . . . that we have ever beheld . . . The views . . . are singularly grand'. Capability Brown was 'improving' the park in 1770.

• • •

bridges, it is not sure whether Brown or Adam designed them. At Claremont, Brown himself was invited by the 1st Lord Clive to rebuild Vanbrugh's earlier mansion, as well as to extend the grounds. His landscaping work, begun in 1768 or 1769, retained most of Kent's earlier design, but re-sited a stretch of the Portsmouth road further to the north, beyond a ridge of rising ground. As for the house, Brown's design was accepted, but in 1770 Brown chose to bring in a partner, the young architect Henry Holland, who was to complete the internal decoration of the house by 1773. He had married Brown's daughter Bridget earlier that year.

HEAVEN'S GATE

In 1770 Brown submitted plans for park and building work at Highclere to Henry Herbert, later Earl of Carnarvon. Highclere was originally a medieval deer park, and had been given formal avenues and garden features in the early eighteenth century. One lengthy lime avenue from this period still leads south towards Beacon Hill. Brown's plans seem to have been accepted, though Herbert had them executed by his own people, and they may have been somewhat modified. The landscaped park at Highclere, with Duns Mere, and spreading vistas from the house out over the Hampshire Downs, still remains much as it was in the 1770s, with classical eye-catchers round the horizon – Jackdaw's Castle, Heaven's Gate, the Rotunda, and the Lake House beside Milford Lake. Some of these buildings were altered by Charles Barry, who drastically remodelled the house in Gothic style in 1839–42. Plantations and belts in Brown's style encircle the parkland, which is notable for its mature, eighteenth-century cedars, and also for early nineteenth-century plantings of hybrid rhododendrons. By 1833, the combination of these plantings with the overall views led J.C. Loudon to write with crushing pomposity

Taking it altogether, then, and considering it as a whole, and with reference both to nature and art, we know of no inland place equal to it.

The early eighteenth-century walled kitchen garden was laid out as as a rose and topiary garden in the present century.

Brown was engaged in 1771–2 at Grimsthorpe, enlarging the lake, and again in Lincolnshire at Brocklesby from 1771, his work extending at intervals until 1780. Though he was consulted here for 'alterations', the state of the gardens and parkland is not certain before his time. He seems to have made a lake from medieval fishponds beside the ruins of Newsham – or Newsome – Abbey, and designed a Gothic bridge, all well to the north of the mansion. Plantations and woodland were laid out extensively southwards from the house, and in this area several buildings were added once the trees were established – the Arabella Aufrère

Temple, the Mary Carter Temple, the Root House and grotto, and the most important feature, the Pelham Mausoleum, by James Wyatt, and built 1787–92. Fine formal terraced gardens, with a geometrical canal, designed by Reginald Blomfield, were reintroduced beside the house in the late 1890s.

A RURAL AIR

At Sheffield Park, in 1776, Brown worked from scratch. John Baker Holroyd, 1st Earl of Sheffield, had an older house drastically remodelled by James Wyatt in 1776–7, and the falling valley landscape below this developing Gothic mansion was Brown's subject. While Sheffield Park is now renowned for its outstanding plantations of trees and shrubs, dating from the later nineteenth century, continued in the early twentieth century, it is proper to remember that Brown 'began' the landscape, creating two lakes at some distance south-eastwards from the

Below: When James Wyatt remodelled the house at Sheffield Park in 1776–7, Capability Brown was called in to create lakes and woodland in the valley below. To his landscape were added two more lakes, and an astonishing richness of trees and shrubs, in the late nineteenth and early twentieth centuries.

. . .

house, and establishing plantations along the boundaries. Repton was consulted in 1789, though it is not clear whether he contributed to the overall design. The two lakes nearer to the house were added a century later.

Brown had been consulted in 1772–3 by the Master and Fellows of St John's College, Cambridge, about a new design for the Wilderness or Fellows' Garden, which he laid out with lawn and encircling trees. Probably as a result of this work he was invited to present a plan for the overall landscaping of the Backs, the area of college and other land on both sides of the river Cam between Magdalene to the north and Queens' College to the south. His plan, dated 1779, was presented, but not implemented. It would have involved a widening of the Cam – not much different from his achievement at Audley End in the mid-1760s – and an opening of the ground on each side of the river to give a rural air to the scene. The project foundered on the intransigence of different colleges, unwilling to abolish the boundaries of their separate holdings along the Cam. While one stretch of the Backs – between the river and King's College – may be said to resemble, approximately, what Brown had proposed, with an area of pasture close to the river, and lawns rising up to the college buildings, the other college gardens are generally enclosed (with their old boundaries), and laid out in formal-cum-floral twentieth-century fashion, seen best in the garden of Trinity Hall, and the Fellows' Garden of Clare.

A fine Brown landscape was planned in the late 1770s at Sledmere for Sir Christopher Sykes, who was noted for his wide-ranging agricultural improvements. Brown's plans were dated 1777–8, and their execution was carried out by Sir Christopher over the next decade. Brown's proposals covered an estate of nearly 2000 acres, removing all trace of earlier straight avenues from the village, and indeed removing the old village itself some distance eastwards and out of sight. The village church however remained, and stands, somewhat isolated, about 400 yards south-east of the house. A winding belt of trees was laid out round the estate boundaries, joined to larger plantations – Avenue Wood, Castle Wood, Cherry Wood. The house itself enjoyed (and still enjoys) wide views outwards over the Yorkshire Wolds, with vistas to two eye-catchers, a classical portico and the Gothic 'Sledmere Castle', built c. 1790. From the south front, the prospect extends over

terraced lawns, past a circular pool, to a serene and spacious – one might say perfect – meadow, rising gently to the wooded horizon. In 1987–8, a formal garden with topiary and box edging was laid out before the west front of the house.

THE DESERTED VILLAGE

To remove a village to make a garden is not uncommon. It happened in seventeenth-century France and England, to clear away obstructions to the grand avenues of formal schemes, and it happened again and again in the eighteenth century, when landscape gardeners, and their patrons, wanted uncluttered 'prospects' out from the mansion, over lawn and lake, valley and woodland. One of the most famous, or notorious, instances was at Nuneham Courtenay, where in 1760–1 the 1st Earl of Harcourt had the old village beside his house demolished, building a new, 'model' village away to the east along the main road to Oxford. It stands there today, and in 1770 Oliver Goldsmith wrote 'The Deserted Village' to commemorate, and lament, such high-handed and inhuman love of nature.

The 1st Earl was his own landscape designer, wanting his new Palladian villa to have a view – the view round from west to north, out to the Thames and up towards Oxford. After the obstructive village had been removed, the medieval village church (which had been left) was pulled down in 1764 and replaced with a building in classical style, designed by the Earl with help from James 'Athenian' Stuart. This building, at once a *church* and a *garden ornament*, was called by Walpole 'the principal feature in one of the most beautiful landscapes in the world'. In 1772, the Earl's son, Lord Nuneham, 'begged an acre' within the grounds for an enclosed, secret, flowery and 'literary' garden. This was designed by William Mason, and described by him in Book IV of *The English Garden* (1781).

On his father's death in 1777, Lord Nuneham, become the 2nd Earl, called in Capability Brown to landscape a further 1000 acres southwest of the house. Brown's plan, submitted in 1779, extended lawns from the house out into the deer park (east of the house), and laid out a winding walk – since called 'Brown's Walk' – southwards through plantations, and with views over the Thames. A Gothic eye-catcher – to be called 'Courtenay Castle' – was intended to complete the southern view, but the proposal was not carried out. In 1786, after Brown's death, the Carfax Conduit, from Oxford, was presented to the Earl, and was erected roughly where the 'ruined castle' would have been.

Brown's landscape swept right up to the front of the house: an expanse of grass, elegantly sprinkled with trees – and moisture, whether dew or raindrops. When Fanny Burney came to stay at Nuneham Courtenay in August 1786, she was disconcerted by the (temporary) absence of the Earl's servants, and by the proximity of Brown's landscape

> We stopped at the portico . . . we were obliged to get out of the carriage by the help of one of (our own) postilions, and to enter the house by the help of wet grass, which would not suffer me to stay out of it.

After his work at Nuneham Courtenay, Brown was still consulted, and many times, but several of his last projects were not executed until after his death in 1783. This applies to his plans for Wilton, supplied in 1779 but which may not have been put into effect; for Althorp, where he gave advice on landscaping in 1780, but where his son-in-law Henry Holland carried out landscaping around 1790 (much modified in the 1860s); and for Stansted, where Brown went to advise twice in 1781 and, possibly, in 1783, the year of his death. Here, landscaping had been under way long before, admired by Horace Walpole in August 1770, 'Most beautifull view from a new Temple, exactly like a Claude Lorrain'. Of the late seventeenth-century avenues, Stansted's great beech vista survives, now enclosed by chestnut woods, and still introduced, as Walpole wrote, by 'very extensive lawns'. Asked pressingly to undertake a landscape commission in Ireland, Brown replied – near the end of his career – that 'he had not yet finished England'.

Left: The Carfax Conduit was brought from Oxford in 1786, and set up here at Nuneham Courtenay as an 'eye-catcher' in the landscape which Capability Brown had laid out in 1779–80. A somewhat similar example of monumental sculpture, the Bristol High Cross, was erected by Henry Hoare at Stourhead in 1765.

• • •

Chapter Five

THE WILDNESS PLEASES

• • •

*B*eside the triumphant spread of Brown's gardens, created from the 1740s until his death in 1783, there are many others by less well-known designers, both professionals and amateurs, which are of immense interest. Broadly speaking, they develop in the mid-century from the earlier style of Kent, and, not unreasonably, often have close affinities with the work of Brown. By the 1770s, the use of numerous classical features, which were so apparent in early landscape gardens, has become more sparing, and the 'landscape' itself is often valued for its rougher and wilder qualities.

LORD BYRON'S ANCESTRAL HOME

Before the mansion lay a lucid Lake,
Broad as transparent, deep, and freshly
    fed
By a river, which its softened way did take
In currents through the calmer water
    spread
Around (*Don Juan*, canto xiii, 1823)

So wrote Byron about his ancestral home, Newstead Abbey. Sir John Byron had acquired the Abbey in 1540, and many of the formal areas are still enclosed by monastic walls. To the west and south of the Abbey, however, the river Leen flows through parkland which had been landscaped in the late 1740s by the 5th Lord Byron. He had made two lakes (a third was added in the mid-nineteenth century), and beside the Upper Lake had built a castellated

'He that mounts the precipices of Hawkstone wonders how he came thither, and doubts how he shall return. His walk is an adventure, and his departure an escape.' Dr Johnson in 1774, but it is as true today of this most 'sublime' of landscape gardens.

• • •

*Above: The ruin or
'folly' at Mount
Edgcumbe is among the
earliest Gothic ruins
erected in Britain,
dating from around
1747. It is sited high up
in the parkland, with
superb views out over
Plymouth Sound.*

• • •

fort and a battery, which, together with 'a great variety of Boats and Ships', enabled him to stage mock battles. 'Two silly forts built', wrote Walpole in 1760. The enclosed garden areas have been much developed in the present century, and informal rock, heather and Japanese gardens have been added further to the south, beside the nineteenth-century Garden Lake.

At Mount Edgcumbe the original house was built in 1547–54, and its site, overlooking Plymouth Sound, was so admirable that in 1588 it was coveted by the Spanish Armada commander, Medina Sidonia, as the place he would claim after England had been subdued. While Mount Edgcumbe, its deer park and its formal gardens did not become Spanish property, it was recognized as an outstanding landscape site in the late 1740s, and its sixteenth- and seventeenth-century features were largely abolished, leaving only the broad Avenue up to the house

from the earlier schemes. By 1747, a Gothic ruin or folly had been erected, itself the most striking architectural feature in the landscape, being on high, open ground visible from far around, and having, I would think, views as splendid as can be found in any garden. They are marine views, out over the hilly parkland to the sea, to Drake's Island, and across to Plymouth and the Devonshire coast. By October 1750, Pococke could write: 'It is by far the finest situation I ever saw, exceeding every thing in the beauty of the near prospects' – and he adds that

the side of the hill [is] planted down . . . to the south, in the face of the very main ocean, where firrs, pines, arbutus, laurustine, and cypress, thrive exceedingly.

Further landscaping took place later in the century, with the idyllically sited Milton's Temple, an Ionic rotunda, standing close to the shore, at the side of the wooded valley called the Amphitheatre, and Thomson's Seat, close to the Lower Gardens.

The area of the Lower Gardens, which had been laid out with a partly formal scheme in the 1730s, was later given several new features – the Orangery, by 1788, with an 'Italian Garden', c. 1799, a 'French Garden' and conservatory, c. 1803–6, and an 'English Garden', possibly inspired by Mason's flower garden at Nuneham Courtenay. Complex floral displays were set out in these areas in the nineteenth century, and also beside the house. After neglect in the 1960s, these have now been renewed.

The park and gardens at Shugborough have exceptional importance in the history of neo-classicism. They were largely formed between 1743 and 1773 for Thomas Anson, with much advice from his brother George Anson, who had circumnavigated the world in 1740–4, and from the architect James 'Athenian' Stuart, author, with Nicholas Revett, of the *Antiquities of Athens* (Vol. I, 1762). Shugborough is the setting for a number of architectural 'firsts' or 'near-firsts' – the Chinese House, 1747, the first European attempt at an accurate replica of a Chinese building; the Doric Temple, c. 1758, second only to the temple of Theseus at Hagley as an example of primitive Doric; the Arch of Hadrian, c. 1761; the 'Lanthorn of Demosthenes', 1764–71, and the Tower of the Winds, c. 1765 – the last three imitating their Athenian originals. Stuart also designed a classical ruin, in about 1748, made more 'ruined' by George Anson, after the workmen had, in their innocence, built it to a more or less complete state: 'Then comes Mr. Anson with axes and chissels to demolish as much of it as taste and judgement claimed.' There are other, lesser monuments scattered over the 400 acres of park and gardens, and others have gone – a pagoda, and a Palladian bridge.

In the late 1790s the park was extended by John Webb, and in 1862 a scheme of formal bedding was laid out in front of the house. This was restored in the late 1960s.

Below: At Shugborough this copy of the Choragic Monument to Lysicrates was erected in the late 1760s. Measured drawings of the original, in Athens, came to England a decade earlier.

• • •

GREAT LAKES AND WATERFALLS

Much of Windsor Great Park had been enclosed by 1086, and its present area of some 5600 acres was achieved by about 1365. In the early 1680s, several imposing avenues were laid out across the heathy terrain, notably the Long Walk, planted with elms for some 2½ miles, replanted in the mid-1940s with plane and chestnut. This superb avenue, beginning at the Cambridge Gate 300 yards south of Windsor Castle, stretches south to the Copper Horse, Westmacott's fine equestrian statue of George III.

In the late 1740s, the southern part of the park was developed by the Duke of Cumberland, who engaged Thomas Sandby to make the lake now called Virginia Water. The first dam was made by 1749, and the triangular Gothic tower, Fort Belvedere, was built, probably by Henry Flitcroft, by 1752 on high ground by the south boundary. The lake was embellished with a 'Chinese' bridge and 'Chinese' fishing temple, and a sizeable 'Chinese' yacht, the *Mandarin*, was towed up the Thames and transported overland to the lake. It was, wrote Mrs Delany in June 1757, 'as rich and gay as carving, gilding and japanning can make it'.

And then, disaster. On 6 September 1768, she wrote again

> I suppose the newspapers have informed you of the extraordinary inundation caused by only one night's rain on Thursday last. The Virginia Water broke head and is entirely gone, fish and all . . .

The breaching of the dam was, in the end, an advantage, for a bigger Virginia Water rose on the site of the first – 130 acres in all, the largest artificial landscape lake in Britain, and given a spectacular cascade in 1782. Close to the southern shore, the classical ruins (composed of columns brought from Leptis Magna) were erected in 1826, and on the northern side of the water, the Valley Gardens were laid out from 1935 onwards with woodland, rhododendron, heather and dwarf conifers.

Further to the north, in the north-eastern sector of Windsor Great Park, the Savill Garden was begun in 1932, and extended in 1950, an area of wild and woodland garden of exceptional interest (see Chapter Seven).

Braxted Park is one of the lesser-known great landscape parks of England. The park and enclosing woodland of some 500 acres included a deer park in the mid-thirteenth century, and Braxted Lodge (as the house was known until around 1848) was given formal gardens in the 1670s, with a triple lime avenue leading southwards. Further avenues were added in the 1750s, radiating from the house, which was rebuilt in this period. Then, in the late eighteenth century, or at the very beginning of the nineteenth, Peter Du Cane enlarged a pool, or pools, westwards from the house, making a glorious lake of 15 acres, with a bridge across the eastern tip, and the strange composite structure of the ice-house-cum-cave-cum-viewing-platform at the western end. Here, in emulation of Painshill, a 'hermit' is supposed to have lived for a year without washing or shaving – for a wager of £100 made by Peter Du Cane.

While the main south avenue has been maintained, the other formal avenues were removed when the lake was created, while extensive and varied plantings of exotic and ornamental trees were made round the west end of the lake, and northwards from the house. The park is private.

William Winde's superb house at Belton, built 1685–8 for Lord Brownlow, was matched by gardens of equal magnificence, with parterres, pools, fountains, statuary and gateways, and avenues leading far across the 680-acre park. Two avenues, to east and south, remain, but mid-eighteenth-century landscaping removed most of the rest, and more was lost around 1778 when William Emes was called in. By 1791, John Byng could write with regret

> For the water works (now destroy'd) I repine; as they must have been curiously imagin'd: and I am rather of opinion that fountains and fanciful water-works are too much discouraged.

The 'landscaping' which replaced the formal features included the Belmont, or Bellmount, Tower, built around 1750 for Lord Tyrconnel at the far end of the eastern avenue, and the area of the Wilderness north-west of Belton House, where the course of the river Witham was adorned with groves enclosing a Gothic ruin, rockwork and a cascade. Of the latter Shenstone was splendidly scornful:

> Surely the *water-fall* is quite detestable. There is something on each side, as I remember, that puts one in mind of a porridge-pot boiling over beneath the pot-lid. (24 November 1759)

Today the cascade is innocuous, and surrounded by intriguingly mixed plantings of yew and bamboo.

Symmetry and formality returned around the house in the nineteenth century. The area of parterres north of the house was re-established in the 1870s with clipped yews, formal bedding patterns and statuary, and a further formal area to the north-west was also laid out, close to Belton church, with the conservatory by Jeffry Wyatville, built in 1819, overlooking a circular pool and fountain.

SCOPE FOR INVENTION

While the layout and landscape design of eighteenth-century gardeners at Kew – Bridgeman and Brown – has been largely overlaid by the work of Nesfield in the 1840s, and by the continuous planting of rare trees and shrubs from the late eighteenth century onwards, some of the buildings designed by Sir William Chambers from this time remain as focal points in the present scheme. The grandiose Orangery is the

earliest, built in 1757 (though dated 1761), and there are also three temples (of Arethusa, 1758; Bellona, 1760; and Aeolus, *c.* 1760, rebuilt in 1845 by Decimus Burton), the Ruined Arch, *c.* 1761 and the Pagoda. He built others which have gone, and their variety called for comment. In September 1761, Walpole tetchily noted 'additions' (he had listed several buildings by 'Chambers the Architect' earlier the same year):

> Little temple at Balbec. Turkish Mosque, very pretty; the dome within ... painted by Wilson with clouds; any body might have done them. A Moorish building; ill-imagined, and I dare say like the buildings of no country. The great Pagoda, 160 feet high, yet sees neither London nor the Thames, nor has one room in it.

At this time, only a small area at Kew, some ten acres, was devoted to botanic specimens. This first area – just south of Chambers' Orangery – was begun in 1759, and it was not until later in the century, under Sir Joseph Banks, and then again in the 1840s, that the botanic aspect of Kew assumed its remarkable significance (see Chapter Six).

Above: If the gardens of Hampton Court were England's answer to Versailles, the lake and cascade at Virginia Water are the response of the English landscape garden to the formal gardens of France. This cascade, formed in 1782, holds in the 'Virginia Water', a modest stream whose waters form Britain's largest eighteenth-century landscape lake.

• • •

CHATSWORTH

• • •

*T*he gardens and park at Chatsworth embody four centuries of development and change. They rank among the world's foremost and most fascinating places, including features from the 1570s to the present day. In the park is Queen Mary's Bower (1570), and up on the rim of the valley is the turreted Stand built around 1581. Within the gardens is Grillet's step cascade, begun around 1696 in the formal style which had come from France.

Then, in the 1750s, the parkland was transformed by Capability Brown, and much of the early formal garden was swept away – only to be reinstated, but with a difference, by Joseph Paxton in the 1830s. He had become the head gardener at Chatsworth in 1826, and was to work for the 6th Duke of Devonshire until the latter's death in 1858.

The diversity of garden development at Chatsworth in the present century is quite as remarkable as its earlier history. Around 1830, Jeffry Wyatville had restored a terrace to the lower side of the gardens, below the west front of Chatsworth House, and here in 1963 a complex parterre design was laid out, based on the ground plan of Lord Burlington's villa at Chiswick. In 1970 the New Greenhouse was built, not far from Paxton's Conservative Wall, while the botanic collections begun in Paxton's time – in the arboretum, the pinetum, the azalea dell and other areas of the gardens – have been decisively enriched since the 1950s.

Round these gardens lies the park, 'diversified' – as the Rev. F.O. Morris wrote in the 1860s – 'with every variety of scenery – the heather-covered hill and sheltered valley, wooded height and gentle slope, the whole studded with majestic trees, the growth of centuries.'

Top right: The canal pond and its fountain unite the early eighteenth century with the nineteenth. Joseph Paxton's Emperor fountain was installed in 1843, in expectation of a visit from Czar Nicholas I. It was the world's tallest gravity-fed fountain.

Right: The 'Great Stove', built by Paxton in the 1830s, was taken down in 1920, but its foundations remain, now enclosing a flower garden.

• • •

Left: The Ring Pond and Serpentine Walks. The hedges, planted in 1953, are now over head height, and reassuringly solid.

Below: The formal gardens on the West Terrace – extensively redesigned in the present century.

• • •

Below: Lake, landscape and mansion at Kedleston survive as one of the principal works of Robert Adam. The 'landscape with lakes', involving the damming of the Cutler Brook, was made in the manner of Brown's 'improvements', which had become famous since the early 1750s.

. . .

ADAM AT KEDLESTON

While Chambers was adding many and varied buildings to the level terrain at Kew, another architect, Robert Adam, was both working on the great house at Kedleston, designing garden buildings, and landscaping the far from level 500-acre park as a whole. In December 1758 he wrote to his brother, James Adam, of the comprehensive nature of his task:

> I . . . got the entire management of the grounds put into my hands, with full powers as to temples, bridges, seats and cascades, so that as it is seven miles around you may guess the play of genius and scope for invention.

Adam's central importance in British neo-classical architecture has obscured his contribution to the landscape garden. Here at Kedleston, however, his talent was employed in a way which – or so I imagine – Brown himself would

have approved. He dammed the Cutler Brook, with six weirs, no less, making a spacious winding 'lake' or 'river', with a couple of islands. The lake is crossed by his bridge (built 1769–70, and set over one of the weirs, with a splendid cascade), and at another point he placed the (combined) bathhouse and boat-houses, surmounted by a fishing room (1761), which ranks among the finest of all garden buildings. As at Nuneham Courtenay, in this period, a village was moved to clear the ground for landscaping. In September 1777, Boswell admired 'the extensive park, with the finest verdure' and 'the large piece of water formed by his Lordship [Lord Scarsdale] from some small brooks, with a handsome barge upon it.' He remarked on this to Johnson:

> One should think (said I,) that the proprietor of all this *must* be happy.' – 'Nay, Sir, (said Johnson,) all this excludes but one evil – poverty.'

Happily, the landscape has survived, with considerable and thoughtful change in the present century, in the region of the house. The Marquess Curzon of Kedleston (1859–1925) remodelled the grounds beside Kedleston Hall, moving several buildings in the process, including an orangery by Adam.

A QUALITY OF WILDNESS

The next four gardens in this chapter are connected by a quality (which those in the seventeenth and early eighteenth centuries would have thought a defect) of *wildness*, which may well (even to some in the twentieth century) take them outside the boundaries of the 'garden', and even beyond the 'park' into the vaguer and unplanned spaces of the 'landscape'. But this was not one of the concerns of those who were then, from about 1750 onwards, eager to

include, or to reach towards some aspect of the *sublime* in nature.

William Aislabie (died 1781), son of John Aislabie the creator of Studley Royal, gardened (if we may use the term) on his own after his father's death in 1742, at Hackfall. The steeply sloping site, some 105 acres, has no house, no visible 'residence'. It is a rocky, wooded ravine, cut through by the river Ure, with points of interest formed by cascades or pools among the tree-clad slopes. Work began around 1750, and by 1751 the peregrinating Richard Pococke was willing to make a two-mile detour 'to see a fine wood of Mr. Aislabie's called Hack-fall', with 'cascades of water . . . tumbling down the hills'. The most beautiful place was 'on a heighth over the river, where there is an octagon Gothick building lin'd with a rock-work of that sort of stone which is commonly called petrifyed moss and roots'. A 'banqueting hall' was built soon

Above: John Aislabie hoped to add the ruins of Fountains Abbey to his property at Studley Royal, but this ambition was not achieved until 1768, long after his death.

. . .

...

after, and an 'eye-catcher' named Mowbray Castle was there before 1772. Today, a wilderness.

By no means a wilderness is the ground enclosing William Aislabie's other acquisition, the ruins of Fountains Abbey. His father had died before he could fulfil his ambition of 'completing' the serene gardens of Studley Royal with the contrasting sublimity of Gothic decay. At last, in 1768, the purchase was concluded. The use of the new property was not, however, to pass without criticism. While John Aislabie had (we may imagine) admired the ruins for their age and dilapidation – in 1682, Ralph Thoresby had remarked that the Abbey ruins were 'now full of trees, within the very body of it' – William Gilpin was to complain in the 1770s that when the new owner had acquired the site, 'his busy hands were let loose upon it', he had added 'ornaments', and now, 'the monks' *garden* is turned into a trim *parterre*'. Gilpin's belief that 'a ruin is a sacred thing' would be tested today, were he to see Fountains Abbey. Secure, stable, yes. But 'ruined'?

The first Thomas Duncombe's ambition, to add to his half-mile terrace at Duncombe Park a further terrace to the west overlooking the ruins of Rievaulx Abbey, was achieved a decade earlier than John Aislabie's at Studley Royal. Around 1758, the third Thomas Duncombe carved out the Rievaulx Terrace, with a Tuscan temple – a rotunda – at the southern end, and an Ionic banqueting house at the northern end. Both were probably designed by Sir Thomas Robinson.

While the Rievaulx Terrace 'echoes' the earlier terrace at Duncombe, with its temples at each end, and its views down to Ryedale, there is here an exceptional and exciting quality which must be identified. The abbey ruins are not seen – as they are at Studley – from a single viewpoint, where the visitor simply comes closer and closer to the object from the same direction. They are viewed *ambulando*, through clearings in the trees which grow on the lower side, as you walk along the broad, grassy terrace, two-thirds of a mile long. The ruins are far below, glimpsed and then lost as you advance round the gently curving lawn. At each point, the view is different, and at the same time, the visitor's relationship (what a pompous word!) to the Ionic or the Tuscan temples on the terrace has changed as well. Arthur Young called it 'moving variation', a term we might use with equal truth and delight, in regarding the tiny Doric temple at Bowood, while walking round Capability Brown's lake.

He that mounts the precipices at Hawkstone, wonders how he came thither, and doubts how he shall return. His walk is an adventure, and his departure an escape.

So wrote Dr Johnson, accompanied by Boswell in 1774, on his one visit to Hawkstone. The site (I dare not call it 'garden') was developed by Sir Rowland Hill (died 1783) and by his son Sir Richard Hill (1733–1809). The extensive lake to the north-west, Hawk Lake, was made by William Emes between about 1783 and 1786, but other garden designers or architects are unnamed. The terrain at Hawkstone is exceptional, since it possesses a huge sandstone bluff, overlooking the level terrain to north, west and south. *In* and *on* this sandstone spur and its related outcrops (Red Castle and Elysian Hill) the Hills, father and son, elaborated a terrace walk, tunnels and monuments. Some features, like the remains of Red Castle (begun 1228), were made more picturesque, and others, like the winding grotto-tunnel within the crest of the sandstone bluff, with its hermitage and (aboveground) Gothic arch, were original. The grotto is unique in Britain, tunnelled *within* the cliff, yet with views *above* the surrounding landscape. 'Above is inaccessible altitude, below is horrible profundity' (Johnson). The hermitage included a hermit, 'the venerable bare-footed Father, whose name is Francis', whose age, 'about 90', remained constant in T. Rodenhurst's *Description of Hawkstone* from 1784 to 1807.

'The ideas which it forces upon the mind are the sublime, the dreadful, and the vast.' Johnson's words were true in 1774, and are true today. We may admire and wonder at Hawkstone – and we may, *reasonably*, think that it is not a garden, just as they did in the 1780s in France, looking at the titanic ruined column in the Désert de Retz, or in Germany, awestruck before the sublime garden volcano at Wörlitz. In England, Hawkstone and its cliff-grotto are the ultimate in 'wildness', the end of nearly a century of search for what is 'natural', in reaction to the excessive formality of Versailles. 'The sublime, the dreadful, and the vast' are not what most garden-lovers, at any period, have desired; and so, towards the end of the eighteenth century, we find another reaction, from wildness to order, and from vastness to modest and comprehensible proportions. The man of the moment will be Humphry Repton.

'CAPABILITY R–'

• • •

Humphry Repton (1752–1818) came to gardening after a quiverful of other occupations. His first serious commission was at Catton Hall (now within the city of Norwich) in 1788, and by the 1790s he had acquired a reputation as the successor to Capability Brown. In 1792, he chanced to meet the peripatetic John Byng, at the Sun Inn, Biggleswade. Though Byng thought well enough of Repton's work, he reckoned that he was somewhat too full of himself, and wrote crossly in his diary

> Mr. Repton – the now noted landscape gardener – came in, and delay'd me for $\frac{1}{2}$ an hour: he is a gentleman I have long known, and of so many words that he is not easily shaken off.

A day later, Byng refers to him as '*Capability R—*'. Though irritable, Byng's remarks catch a fair amount of the truth – Repton was indeed 'noted', and he was noted as the one landscape gardener with talent enough to carry on where Brown had stopped. 'Carry on' he did, often literally, since many of the parks and gardens where he worked had already been landscaped by Brown, or in the manner of Brown, having been given broad, grassy sweeps round the house, water in the middle distance, and belts of trees on the horizon.

For many, though not all, of his commissions, Repton gave his clients a bound volume (in red morocco) with his proposals – handwritten text, with suggestions and notes, and delicately executed plans and views to illustrate his ideas. These beautifully presented proposals, known as Red Books, survive in large numbers, in some instances for schemes which the clients may not in the end have implemented, or only in part. Nearly always, they contain one or more views which indicate (by means of a folding flap of paper) the state of the site as Repton found it, and what it would be like if his 'improvements' were carried out.

We should note that Repton not only landscaped many sites which had been developed to some extent already but that his work was often overlaid or altered in turn. This has been the case at Thoresby, where an elaborate formal scheme from the 1680s was 'softened' early in the next century, and Thoresby Lake was formed from the river Meden. Further landscaping took place in the 1780s, and Brown is

thought to have been involved – at least from a phrase by Repton in 1803: 'I shall have occasion to propose a different idea to that suggested by Mr. Brown'. Repton himself had been called in some while before – his Red Book is dated 1791 – and his work involved redesigning the cascade which ended Thoresby Lake, and extending the 'serpentine' character of the stream. While the lake and cascade remain in the broad parkland, much of the area north-east of the lake was transformed in the mid-1860s, when the present house was built by Anthony Salvin, and an imposing terraced garden overlooking the park was laid out. W.A. Nesfield produced designs in 1863, but the garden may be Salvin's work. It is resolutely formal, with sculpture, stone-edged beds, and patterns of massed bedding set in a symmetrical design – and characteristic of the widespread reaction against 'natural' landscaping which took place in nineteenth-century gardens.

Repton produced another Red Book for Port Eliot in 1792. Here again, eighteenth-century

landscaping had brought about the infilling of a large creek northwards from the house (it had extended to the eastern boundary, formed by the curving course of the river Tiddy), and the creation of a lake further to the north. Repton's work, for the 1st Lord Eliot, effectively resulted in additional plantings of trees round the boundaries of the park, and the elaboration of a riverside walk, bounded in the nineteenth century by the Boathouse and the Battery to north and south. A dairy, which may have been designed by Sir John Soane, was built on the northern shore of the lake in Repton's time. Repton may have been involved in developing paths in the woodland east of the house, which was much altered by the addition of flowering shrubs in the mid-nineteenth century.

Brown's grand plan for the Backs at Cambridge had been a failure. So was Repton's, with one of his most splendid Red Books, for the landscaping of the grounds of Magdalen College, Oxford. His proposals were invited by the Fellows of the College in 1801, and his response

was both ambitious and ill-considered. He proposed the remodelling of much of the quad, the removal of the entire east side, and the landscaping of the ground eastwards, to the river Cherwell, and on the further side. Repton was only dealing with a single college, but the varied and established interests of the Fellows were sufficient to ensure the rejection of his scheme.

At Woburn, in contrast, Repton's proposals for the 6th Duke of Bedford were triumphantly successful. 'The Improvements I have had the honour to suggest have nowhere been so fully realised as at Woburn Abbey', he wrote, after many years of involvement. He was called in by the 6th Duke in 1804, and his Red Book was produced in January 1805. One of his finest, it contains no less than 47 illustrations.

Woburn is, like so many of the grander estates in this history, a site of great historic complexity. After earlier developments, mentioned in Chapter One, the parkland was landscaped in the second half of the eighteenth

Above: The view of the house at Port Eliot from the northern side parkland landscaped by Humphry Repton in the closing years of the eighteenth century.

• • •

• • •

century, and the size of the estate – some 3000 acres – allowed the creation of varied yet unclashing features. When Count Kielmansegge was there in 1762, he saw one lake with a 'Chinese pavilion', and another, 'close to the house', with 'a fine yacht of thirty to forty tons, carrying ten guns, with other smaller boats', to be paralleled at West Wycombe, or Virginia Water, in the same period.

Henry Holland had already designed the Chinese Dairy to the north-east of Woburn Abbey in the 1790s, before Repton was engaged. In the region eastwards from the Abbey, Repton designed and saw the creation of a group of linked yet separate areas: a rosary, an American and a Chinese garden, a menagerie and an aviary. These were mainly completed by about 1810, as well as the reshaping of the lakes westwards from the Abbey, and the related re-routing of the southern approach drive. The *variety* of these areas and features is characteristic of Repton's understanding that his clients now wanted, not simple 'landscape' around their property, but landscapes and gardens of contrasting – and intriguingly different – characteristics. Much garden development in the nineteenth century will follow his example.

Apparently satisfied with Repton's work at Woburn, the 6th Duke of Bedford asked him to advise on the development of one of his remoter estates, at Endsleigh in Devon. Here the ground had not been 'gardened' or 'landscaped' at all,

and Repton (in conjunction with Jeffry Wyatt, who was to design the house) was first asked to submit proposals in 1809. While Repton's Red Book was dated September and October 1814, much of the landscape scheme, and all of Wyatt's buildings, had been completed by this time.

The site at Endsleigh is outstanding – a steeply sloping property, overlooking the deep, curving course of the Tamar, with thick woodland all round, and magnificent views out over the valley. It is wild, forested country, as Repton said:

> Here, Solitude, embosomed in all the sublimity of umbrageous majesty looks down on the infant River struggling through its rocky channel . . .

Yet his landscaping was not wild, and there is no touch of Hawkstone at Endsleigh. Instead Repton created two most admirable and regular terraces, one to the south-west of the cottage, with a Children's Garden and fountain, and the other, longer, to the south-east, leading to the Shell House and grotto. Beyond is the Swiss Cottage, c. 1810. While his other proposals, also executed, included plantations along the approach, and the planting of rare and exotic trees

northwards from the cottage (now Endsleigh House), and several buildings of a rustic nature to the west, we should note the Children's Garden and fountain mentioned above. For most of a century, fountains and formal gardens had been out of fashion, seen by their fiercest critics as 'against nature' and therefore *wrong* – no less. Now, discreetly, Repton brought them back. They overlook a wild and convincingly natural valley, but, in themselves, Repton's fountain, and his circular bedding divided into regular segments, are as formal as anything from Versailles.

Repton was involved to a lesser (and sometimes uncertain) degree in many of the gardens or parks discussed in this book – at Bowood, for example, Brocklesby, Harewood, Holkham, Longleat, Sheffield Park, West Wycombe and Wimpole. Only at Sezincote should his contribution be mentioned in any detail, where he was probably engaged between about 1804 and 1805, and then in conjunction with the artist Thomas Daniell, at the same time as the house was being built (for Sir Charles Cockerell) by his brother Samuel Pepys Cockerell. It is thought (though without absolute proof) that Repton was responsible for the lake, east and downhill from the house, which overlooks the parkland

Above: Repton's long arcaded terrace at Endsleigh, backed by the yew walk, is one of the landmarks in the return of formality to garden design. Laid out between 1810 and 1814, the gardens at Endsleigh have superb views out over the wooded valley of the Tamar.

• • •

Above: At Sezincote, the house, including this curving orangery wing, was built around 1805 by S.P. Cockerell with advice from the artist and traveller Thomas Daniell. Daniell had spent several years in India, and his views of Indian architecture were influential both in the house and gardens at Sezincote, and at Brighton, in Nash's designs for the Royal Pavilion.

• • •

from a ha-ha; and that he sited the belts of woodland round parts of the estate. He also drew a sketch for a small flower garden, but the gardens near to the house, built in a distinctive 'Indian' style, are more firmly attributable to Daniell, who had (with his nephew William) been involved in the travels and topographical illustrations in India which led to their six-volume *Oriental Scenery* (1795–1808). At Sezincote, Thomas Daniell designed the eight-sided fountain, the sundial and the grotto south of the house, and, in the ornamental woodland to the north, the Indian Bridge, with shrine upstream, and the Snake Pool and bronze three-headed serpent downstream. Both these areas – the garden south of the house and the woodland and stream garden to the north – have been extensively restored and remodelled since 1944, with advice from G.S. Thomas, the south garden having been given a more distinctively 'Indian' look, with Irish yews emphasizing the axial paths round the fountain, and an Indian pavilion on the south side, while the woodland garden has been enriched with flowering shrubs and trees.

Repton's contact with Thomas Daniell had begun before their work together at Sezincote. Around 1803, Repton had prepared a Red Book (presented in 1808), with 'Designs for the Pavilion at Brighton', in which he acknowledged the 'new source of richness and variety,

new grace and beauty in the designs of Mr. Thomas Daniell'. Repton's proposals for the grounds and garden buildings at Brighton were not accepted, and instead, after a lengthy interval, the Prince Regent preferred designs by John Nash – who had, until 1799, worked in collaboration with Repton on several house-and-garden projects.

NASH'S LONDON

Nash, like Robert Adam, is thought of primarily as an architect, yet – like Adam at Kedleston – he is also responsible for important landscape designs. Regent's Park was designed by Nash (plan 1811, executed, with modifications, between 1812 and about 1830), and the public area of the park was opened in 1835, five years after Nash's death. The 470 acres of this roughly circular site are enclosed by roads, and also, on the northern side, by a mile of the Grand Union Canal, constructed 1812–20. Nash's first plan proposed the building of many separate villas and elegant terraces of houses inside the landscaped grounds, but by the 1830s these ideas were modified. Terraces were built round some outer parts, and a few private villas – including St John's Lodge and Holme House – were sited on the outer side of the Inner Circle. This area, the Inner Circle, was acquired in 1835 by the Royal Botanic Society for its gardens, and was developed from 1932 onwards as Queen Mary's Gardens, with a rose garden, and with an open air theatre. In 1827, a large part of the northern quarter of the site was acquired by the Royal Zoological Society, and some 60 acres are now used as the Regent's Park Zoo.

In garden and landscape terms, Nash created a great circular park, with houses built, or intended to be built, all round. To the left, or west of the Inner Circle and its connecting roads, a large three-pronged lake was made, whose shape resembles 'to use a simile more accurate than dignified, the arrangement of the three legs on an Isle of Man halfpenny', according to Nathan Cole in 1877, in *The Royal Parks and Gardens of London*. He added that the east side of the park was 'very tastefully laid out, showing both the English and the Italian style. The English consists in an imitation of nature.' While the 'English' style remains in the grassy areas of lawns, with clumps of trees, and possibly in the many fields, pitches and lesser areas set aside for sport, the 'Italian' style remains, sketchily, along the north–south length of the Broad Walk, with fine displays of massed bedding, between noble lines of horse chestnuts.

St James's Park, laid out formally for Charles II in 1661, had declined indeed by 1782, when the German traveller Moritz was there. It was 'formed of an alley of trees, which enclose a large green area, in the middle of which is a marshy pond.' There were cows, and one could buy fresh milk. Brown had already proposed a landscape layout in the 1760s, and his plan was, at last, largely adopted by Nash in 1828–9. The long straight canal (Moritz's 'marshy pond') became the softly contoured lake, with an island at each end, surrounded by undulating lawns and curving paths. Nash's work was helped, for the planting, by William Aiton, of Kew. By 1835, Jonas Dennis in *The Landscape Gardener* could write 'Certainly considerable credit redounds to the projector of these improvements . . . in converting a Dutch canal into a fine flowing river.' St James's Park has also become a 'fine flowing *corridor*', absorbing thousands and thousands of pedestrians, and concealing most of them from each other as they cross from the Mall to Birdcage Walk, saunter along the serpentine paths, linger by the bridge, or sit, wondering who may sit next to them, on the park benches. In 1983, Hunter Davies wrote with truth that St James's Park was 'the haunt of Civil Servants'.

Left: Nash's design for St James's Park was executed in 1828–9, though the essential design had been proposed by Capability Brown long before.

• • •

Chapter Six

GARDENS OLD AND NEW

• • •

*T*he variety of gardens created in the first quarter of the nineteenth century reflects the interest, and indeed eagerness of many owners to escape from the supposed monotony of the lake-with-rolling-parkland common in the 1790s. While Sezincote turned to an 'Indian' style, Belsay, in remote Northumberland, embraced an austere form of Greek revival architecture in the house, built from 1807 to 1817 for Sir Charles Monck. From Belsay Hall, high, almost cliff-like terraces and an arched ha-ha overlook a valley landscape with lake, and the quarry garden, laid out apparently by Monck himself in the rugged spaces left after the stone had been extracted for Belsay Hall. Though the rockwork with the gorge and natural 'bridge' may be as jagged and wild as that of Hawkstone, the vegetation – helped, to be true, in the later nineteenth century, by further plantings – is luxuriant and varied, with areas of contrasting yew, rhododendron and laburnum.

If the gorge, arch and vegetation at Belsay are distinctively 'different' from the surrounding northern countryside, the many buildings and garden structures in the steep valley of the Churnet stream below Pugin's castellated Alton Towers are even stranger, since they are of such oddly separated styles. Between 1814 and 1837 the 15th and 16th Earls of Shrewsbury built one of the most bizarre collections of buildings any garden has ever contained. Though ample – and well-judged – plantings of bushes and trees by Alexander Forsyth in the 1840s and later did

Though the planting has been much simplified, the architectural *splendour of Sir Charles Barry's steps and balustrades at Shrubland Park, created in 1848–52, remains as one of the most ambitious of Italianate garden schemes.*

• • •

Right: The rock arch, in the quarry garden at Belsay, is in the sublime tradition of the Gothic ruin in the parkland at Mount Edgcumbe, or the cliff-edge grotto tunnels of Hawkstone. But its surrounding planting of rhododendrons indicates the changing interests of the nineteenth century.

. . .

much to separate these features, the assemblage remains peculiar: Gothic – the mansion itself and a three-storeyed tower, in cast iron; prehistoric (a form of Stonehenge); Greek (the Choragic monument to Lysicrates); a Roman bridge; a Swiss cottage (for a blind harper, no less); a conservatory of Moorish or Brighton-pavilion-inspired kind; and, most famous of all, the three-storeyed Chinese pagoda, by Robert Abraham, built in 1827 in cast iron, and with a fountain jet at the top. As J.C. Loudon wrote in 1831, in the *Gardener's Magazine*:

> Such a labyrinth of terraces . . . vases, statues, . . . bridges, porticoes, pagodas, gates, iron railings, parterres, jets, ponds, streams, seats, fountains, caves, flower baskets [and 13 more items, ending with '&c'] that it is utterly impossible for words to give any idea of the effect.

Uphill from the gardens of Alton Towers are now their modern equivalent in variety and popular appeal: a pleasure park with roller-coaster and comparable delights.

'NEW' RESTORATIONS

The eclectic – or jackdaw's nest – approach at Alton Towers was generally much less common than a simpler historicism, an attempt to reproduce no more than *one* 'historical' style in the garden area close to the house. Dissatisfaction with the overall landscape approach of the previous century – the grass-right-up-to-the-door which had so distressed Fanny Burney at Nuneham Courtenay – led most often to the architectural 'extension' of the house itself by means of a terrace, or its visual equivalent. Whether the terrain was sloping or level, an area before the house would be given rectangular shape, and enclosed by balustrades or lines of urns. If the ground sloped away, and if the house was grand enough, steps would lead down to a further terrace, still aligned on the house, and with the central axis extending outwards between symmetrical arrangements of sculpture, urns, fountains, the whole made colourful by different floral schemes, and given green vertical emphasis by means of topiary or pergolas with climbing plants.

At a glance, this description might imply a return to the formal gardens of Versailles, no more. But the creators of these gardens, from the early 1800s onwards, imagined a much more varied historical approach. As early as 1806, on 24 December, William Wordsworth was writing to Lady Beaumont to suggest she make a small, trellis-enclosed 'winter garden' modelled on the description in the late medieval poem 'The Flower and the Leaf' – 'shut up within a double and tall fence of evergreen shrubs and trees', with box-edged flowerbeds, and a fountain, and in his Red Book of 1814 for Beaudesert, in Staffordshire, Humphry Repton proposes that the mid-sixteenth-century mansion should be given a formal, terraced flower garden in harmony with the house's 'pristine character'. He had obtained antiquarian help for this project, and had it been executed, it would have been the earliest serious attempt at historical garden reconstruction in the nineteenth century. A few years earlier, in 1808, Repton had stated categorically in his 'Designs for the Pavilion at Brighton' that 'Gardens are works of art rather than nature', and the 'art' which was now more and more frequently sought out, to keep the dullness of nature away from the house, was that of previously established (if only partially understood) garden styles. A century later, the collection of *Country Life* articles on British

Left: The pagoda at Alton Towers, built in 1827, is both the most striking and the most intriguing of the many garden features. Obviously 'Chinese' in its form, it is none the less essentially British (and un-Chinese) in its cast-iron construction, and with a fountain at the top.

• • •

gardens by H. Avray Tipping, *Gardens Old and New*, describes and illustrates a galaxy of 'French', 'Dutch', 'Elizabethan', 'Spanish' and above all 'Italian' gardens, nearly all made or refurbished in the course of the nineteenth century. They are therefore 'new', but their owners most often believed, or claimed, that they were 'old', being a restoration of what *had* been there centuries before, or what *might have been* if their new mansion in Gothic, Tudor or

Renaissance style had really been built that long ago.

An Italian Renaissance

The most popular appellation was 'Italian', and one of the best early examples was at Wilton, on the west side of the house. Here in 1820–1, Catherine, Countess of Pembroke had Sir Richard Westmacott's design laid out, with

around 1830, bringing formal gardens from the house right down to the landscape lake (which had been made, probably by Stephen Wright, by damming the river Poulter in 1774–89), so that his balustrades overlooked the water; and at Audley End, where on the east side his axial flower garden lies between the house and the ha-ha, 'distancing' Brown's landscape from the house. At Clumber, the house was destroyed in 1938, and the terraces stand houseless and – I think – forlorn; though his formal avenue to the north-east, with four parallel rows of limes is still a magnificent, three-mile prelude to the view of the lake. At Audley End, his layout was much modified later in the nineteenth century, and restoration is now in progress.

These 'Italian' or 'French' schemes continue with increasing assurance – at Wrest Park, as we have already seen in Chapter Two, around 1835; at Chatsworth a terraced garden area was laid out by Wyatville around 1830 (its *present* parterre scheme was devised as recently as 1963); at Bowood the terrace south of the stable courts was built for the 3rd Marquess of Lansdowne by Sir Robert Smirke in 1817–18, fountains were added in 1839, and the lower terrace was laid out by George Kennedy by 1853. The details have since been changed on several occasions, but Kennedy's general scheme has been faithfully maintained.

In the 1840s, Lewis Vulliamy is thought to have designed terraces for Westonbirt House, Gloucestershire (their exact date is uncertain, since he had remodelled R.S. Holford's original house in 1839, before replacing it with the present house, now Westonbirt School, in 1863–70). These terraces stretch the whole width of the house, and extend to the south in three stages, for some 300 yards. The lowest terrace is 200 yards in length. Eastwards, at the end of the upper terrace, is the Italian Garden (curiously Moorish in its sculptural style, but Italian it is called), for which some drawings by Vulliamy's pupil, H.E. Hamlen, are dated 1843. Though the Italian garden is partly enclosed, both it and the main terraces have fine views out to the southern parkland, planted (like the terraces) with superb trees from the 1840s onwards.

From the 1840s until the 1860s, garden after garden was adorned with parterres, often edged with stone and enclosed with balustrades, to overlook the parkland made 'natural' in the previous century. Being indeed an architectural form of gardening, they were often designed by

Left: These terraced gardens were laid out at Bowood in the nineteenth century, and their present form was achieved in 1864. Though some of the bedding has been simplified, they remain as a fine example of Victorian 'Italianate' style.

• • •

profuse additions of statuary round a central fountain and stone-edged flower beds. At the far, western end of the axis is the Holbein Porch, which had earlier been the sixteenth-century entrance to the house from the north side of the courtyard, and was moved here in the early 1800s.

William Sawrey Gilpin (1762–1843), nephew of the Rev. William Gilpin, designed several terraced areas in this manner – at Clumber

Right: This lovely pond and fountain both enclose the Italian Garden at Westonbirt House, and allow views out from the formal garden area to the southern parkland, in the manner of a ha-ha wall. The Italian Garden was probably designed in the 1840s, and the first plantings of ornamental trees in the park may have been somewhat earlier.

Opposite below: Superb examples of two garden styles are united here at Harewood House: the undulating landscape, laid out in the mid- and later eighteenth century, and the formal terraces added round three sides of the house by Sir Charles Barry in the 1840s.

. . .

architects – such as Sir Charles Barry (1795–1860) – who would leave the floral in-filling of the beds to the head gardener. In this way, when Barry remodelled Harewood House, he also laid out the splendid terrace garden in 1844–8, with the help of the gardener John Fleming. At Harewood, the upper terrace is linked with the house by a grand double stairway, and the use of elaborate stairs, single or double, with related balustrades, statuary and fountains, was gladly adopted if the site was steep enough.

The models were consciously Italian, and theatrical – the Villa Torrigiani, for instance, or the Villa Garzoni, both near Luccia and laid out in the seventeenth century. The most ambitious examples are Osborne House on the Isle of Wight and Barry's vast creation at Shrubland Park. Osborne, laid out by Thomas Cubitt between 1847 and 1853 for Prince Albert, was to some extent designed by Prince Albert himself, who, like Barry, had made long visits to central and northern Italy. At Shrubland in Suffolk, where the house had been remodelled in 1830–2 by J.P. Gandy-Deering, and given a fine conservatory and an upper terrace, Barry was called in by Sir William Middleton to give an 'Italianate' finish to the house, and to implement Gandy-Deering's earlier and unexecuted garden plans. In the event, Barry's scheme (1848–52) carried four successive flights of steps – 115 steps in all – from the upper house terrace down to the main terrace-garden, the Panel Garden. Here the circular fountain and parterres are enclosed by balustrades, and the axis of the steps is completed by a three-arched loggia, overlooking the further view into the park. The terrace of the Panel Garden extended to either side for most of a mile, with several separate features, including a 'Chinese' garden, a 'French' garden and a maze. Though many of the smaller elements at Shrubland have declined, the architectural centre of steps and Panel Garden survive in virtually complete form.

Barry was also responsible for giving the great parterre at Cliveden its decisive form in 1851, again with the planting advice of John Fleming. The Cliveden scheme was enriched by Lord Astor in the mid-1890s with the lower terrace and Borghese balustrade beneath the

upper terrace, and with the sculpture of Pluto and Persephone at the southern end of the parterre.

George Devey's restoration of the gardens at Penshurst Place dates from about 1850. Keeping to the main lines of the sixteenth- and seventeenth-century plan, his main work was the recreation of a formal parterre – the Italian Garden – which has been maintained with slight variation ever since.

William Andrews Nesfield (1793–1881), a

Below: The Italianate scheme at Osborne House, laid out by Thomas Cubitt for Prince Albert. The strong axial emphasis of pool, path and steps conceals the slope of the ground, falling from right to left.

• • •

contemporary of Barry, may possibly have worked with him at Harewood, though other cooperation is uncertain. He designed the terraces at Holkham, in 1849, which are his best surviving work. His intricate *parterres de broderie* at Castle Howard round the Atlas Fountain were replaced in the 1890s with the present layout of yew hedges and lawn. Similarly at Drayton House, Nesfield's parterre to the east, made in 1846, was replaced by lawn in the present century. At Witley Court, in Herefordshire, his terraces and huge stone-edged beds, with James Forsyth's two sculptured fountain groups, lie like garden skeletons before the shell of the mansion, burnt out in 1937.

Frequently the patterns of the parterres included the representation of heraldic features (as did the topiary), or the initials of the family. The letter H was at one point to have been part of the parterre at Harewood; at Bowood Kennedy's original design included cut monograms and coronets; at Castle Ashby, when terraces were laid out in 1860–5, designed by Sir Digby Wyatt, the designs for the parterres, by the

Marquess of Northampton himself, incorporated the family monogram; and at Hardwick, where the letters ES form a prominent part of the sixteenth-century balustrading of the house, historicism in gardening resulted in a massive ES in ribbon bedding in the forecourt. This pattern has long since been grassed over, but in dry summers its ghost shows through.

Likewise grassed over, but retaining urns and columnar yews are W.M. Teulon's terraced gardens at Althorp, to the north and east of the house. These were laid out in 1860 for the 5th Earl Spencer, and the line of Teulon's balustrade is continued round the south side of the house with stone pillars and ironwork, to separate the forecourt from the park.

Most strongly architectural, and also 'Italian' in its nature, is the area at the north end of the Long Water in Kensington Gardens. Here in the 1860s an entirely stone-built scheme of pavilions, paved terraces, fountains, sculpture and balustrades was made overlooking Kent's lake. It could have come from Osborne – or Italy. Kensington Gardens, one of the royal

parks and gardens, may be matched in this development with the sudden and remarkable emergence of the first 'public park', Birkenhead Park, which was designed and laid out in 1843–7 by Joseph Paxton and Edward Kemp. Round the park were built a number of entrance lodges, in styles as varied as the mansions of mid-Victorian England – Norman, Gothic, Italian, Castellated – while the grandiose principal entrance was in Ionic style. Within the park were a Swiss bridge, and another in cast iron. But all this, important enough, was less potent than Paxton's overall design, which involved the creation of a space free from the sight of urban development. He enclosed the park in clumps and belts of trees, round a peripheral drive (though he accepted areas of housing round the park, and beside parts of the central dividing road); and with the spoil from lakes excavated in the western and eastern halves, hillocks and ridges were made to divide the park into genuinely 'private' areas of lawn, lake and woodland resembling the countryside. The young American, Frederick Law Olmsted, was

as impressed by the landscaping – which he reproduced in New York's Central Park – as he was by the politics of it all. His visit, in 1850, was related in 1852 in his *Walks and Talks . . . in England*, where he said

All this magnificent pleasure-ground is entirely, unreservedly, and for ever the people's own . . . Is it not a grand good thing?

HOUSES FOR PLANTS

By this time other changes, themselves immense, had taken place in the English garden. The development of the greenhouse or conservatory might be thought a strictly architectural matter, yet the siting of these buildings was often prominent within the garden, and their role was of the greatest importance in furthering the collection and successful growth of species newly introduced from abroad. There had of course been rooms, or buildings, made for the 'conservation' of tender plants in the winter

Above: Where a formal layout with long avenues had been 'landscaped' in the late eighteenth century by Brown or his followers, the house was often left in a sea of lawn and parkland. At Althorp this situation was changed in 1860–3, when Teulon laid out a complex framework of parterres and lawns, with balustrades, railings and piers round most of the house.

• • •

months, since at least the sixteenth century – often called 'stoves', since they were primarily *heated* rooms, to protect plants against the cold. The idea of admitting maximum *light* was not clearly understood until much later, and many of the large and elaborate 'orangeries' built in the second half of the eighteenth century (such as Chambers' Orangery at Kew), intended for the winter housing of citrus fruit, still have very much more wall than glass.

The appreciation of the need for light as well as warmth is splendidly apparent at Bicton. While the late eighteenth-century orangery, the Temple, at the upper end of the formal garden, is still firmly classical in its architectural style, the Palm House, nearby to the west, is impressively a 'glass house' – the earliest example in Britain. It was built around 1820. Much larger, and with a soaring dome, is the Great Conservatory at Syon Park, built for the 3rd Duke of Northumberland by Charles Fowler between 1827 and 1830. Fowler also designed the strictly formal flower garden on the south side of his new building.

Most influential of these conservatories was that at Chatsworth, the Great Stove, built in 1836–40 by Joseph Paxton for the 6th Duke of Devonshire. J.C. Loudon visited Chatsworth several times, and in May 1839 he wrote enthusiastically about the 'many improvements' he had seen:

> The most remarkable is the erection of a large tropical conservatory. In general design it may be compared to a cathedral with a central aile and side ailes . . . it will cover above an acre and a quarter of ground. There will be a carriage drive through it . . . it is unquestionably the largest structure of the kind in existence or on record.

After his next visit, in May 1840, Loudon announced triumphantly in the *Gardener's Magazine*: 'at present the glazing is almost completed'. The Great Stove, one of the wonders of the garden world, lasted until 1920. Its site is now occupied by a maze, created in the 1970s.

Joseph Paxton (1803–65) has already been mentioned in connection with Birkenhead Park. In 1826 he was appointed head gardener at Chatsworth, and remained in the 6th Duke's service until the latter's death in 1858, though undertaking important outside commissions and becoming a public figure in his own right.

His work at Chatsworth covered many aspects of these complex gardens. As well as the Great Stove, now gone, he built the Conservative Wall, a series of glass 'rooms' or 'cases' against a long, pre-existing wall, which still remain. He created the Emperor Fountain (1843), in its time the tallest jet in the world, and from the 1830s onwards he planted the pinetum and the arboretum. So famous was his Great Stove that in 1850 he was asked to design the exhibition hall for the Great Exhibition of 1851. The building – the Crystal Palace – was erected in Hyde Park to the south of the Serpentine, and Paxton was knighted in recognition of his work. In 1852–3 the Crystal Palace was dismantled and reassembled triumphantly at a new site, Sydenham Hill in south London, since known as Crystal Palace Park. It was destroyed by fire in 1936, though Paxton's huge terraces remain.

It is proper to mention the dismantling and reassembling of the Crystal Palace, since its materials – cast iron and sheet glass – were products of the continuing industrial revolution. In the middle years of the century, technical advances, such as James Hartley's patenting of the sheet glass process (1847) coincided with important fiscal changes, such as the abolition of the glass tax in 1845, and of the brick tax in 1850. The rapid building of conservatories – or 'glass houses' – had therefore become technically simpler and, relatively, less costly than before.

Between Paxton's Great Stove and the Crystal Palace comes the Palm House at Kew. Designed by Richard Turner and Decimus Burton, and built in 1844–8, it is, like the far smaller Palm House at Bicton, a superb example of functional architecture. Its curvilinear outline, its wholly-glazed exterior are patently intended for the housing and display of large, tender *plants* – and not pretending in any way to echo the shape or features of a classical or Gothic building whose aim is to house *people*. That, in 1850–1, was the avowed purpose of the Crystal Palace – to house the products of the world and the myriads of people who would come to see them. By 1859–62, when Decimus Burton's Temperate House was built at Kew (it was extended in 1898–9), his design was weaker, and he produced, not another or a better Palm House, but a smaller Crystal Palace. The Temperate House is a grand building, and in its recently restored splendour has aspects of fairy-tale abode – but it does not declare unequivocally 'Here is a house for plants'.

Opposite: The Palm House at Bicton, built around 1820. One of the earliest surviving 'glass houses' in Britian (as opposed to the earlier 'orangeries', a fine example of which may also be seen at Bicton), it is clearly functional in its design, heralding the perfection of form achieved in the Palm House at Kew.

* * *

THE GREAT TREE COLLECTIONS

From the 1820s onwards the building of new, large conservatories for tender plants is paralleled by the establishment of collections of trees and shrubs, sometimes in a particular area of a garden, sometimes scattered over the garden and parkland generally. Since the later eighteenth century, plant hunters had found and brought back to Britain an increasing number of specimens from China, Japan, the western parts of North America, and Australasia, and the development of an *arboretum* was an obvious extension of this newly acquired botanic treasure. When the Wardian case (a sealed, glazed plant case, invented, or discovered, by the perceptive Dr Nathaniel Bagshaw Ward in 1829) enabled small growing plants to be brought safely back, the rate of successful plant introductions rose dramatically.

It is not possible to list here, or to celebrate, the discoveries or the discoverers of these species, but it will be instructive to list, crudely and without detail, some of the trees or shrubs which came to this country between the 1730s and the 1890s. Many of them now appear so often, so easily, in our gardens that they seem 'native' – but they are not:

Magnolia (*c.* 1730); Witch hazel (1736); Tree of Heaven (1751); Maidenhair tree (1754); Lombardy poplar (1758); Tree paeony (1789); Hydrangea (1789); Monkey puzzle (1795); Kerria (1805); Wistaria (1816); Mahonia (1827); Forsythia (*F. viridissima*, 1844, *F. suspensa*, *c.* 1850); Winter jasmine (1844); Berberis (*B. darwinii*, 1849); Cotoneaster (1879); Russian vine (*c.* 1890); Buddleia (*B. davidii*, 1896).

KEW
The Royal Botanic Gardens

• • •

*T*he three hundred acres of the Royal Botanic Gardens at Kew have assumed their status as the world's foremost botanic gardens in gentle stages. Today, the throng of visitors will be aware, above all, of the overwhelming variety and richness of the collected species, whether outside, or under glass in the several conservatories, or preserved among the six million specimens in the herbarium. Yet when in 1759 Princess Augusta, the Dowager Princess of Wales, set aside some ten acres of her gardens (no more!) for botanic collections, the rest of her grounds were simply ornamental and kitchen gardens. Nor did she control all the present 300 acres, since the southern area was a separate royal property, which Bridgeman had laid out for Queen Caroline. 'Landscaping' of the two gardens continued separately for some time, with Sir William Chambers at work for Princess Augusta, and Capability Brown 'improving' the southern area for George III. The properties were united in 1772, on the death of Princess Augusta.

By this time, the importance of the original botanic collection was considerable, and notable enthusiasts were involved. The head gardener, William Aiton, had been advised by Lord Bute until 1772, and the unofficial directorship of the botanic collection then came to Sir Joseph Banks, President of the Royal Society.

The greatest expansion of Kew as a centre for botanic research dates from 1841, when the gardens were made a public research institute. Sir William Hooker was the first director, W.A. Nesfield undertook the landscaping of the grounds, and Decimus Burton, with Richard Turner, designed the Palm House (built 1844–8). A sign of the continuing pre-eminence of the Royal Botanic Gardens is the creation of new glasshouses in the 1980s – the Alpine House (opened 1981) and the Tropical Conservatory (Princess of Wales Conservatory, opened 1987).

Right: 'Gardens old and new' are a continuing part of the tradition at Kew. The sunken herb garden was begun in 1964, and contains a kaleidoscopic array of plants long known for their 'herbal' properties.

• • •

118

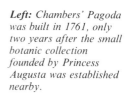

Left: *Chambers' Pagoda was built in 1761, only two years after the small botanic collection founded by Princess Augusta was established nearby.*

Below: *The simple curving lines of the Palm House – designed by Decimus Burton and Richard Turner (1844–8) – reveal its supremely functional design – to admit as much light as possible to the exotic plants within.*

• • •

Among the enthusiasts for these collections of trees was William Sawrey Gilpin. At Westonbirt, he is thought to have advised R.S. Holford (1806–92) on the laying out of his parkland, even before Vulliamy was engaged to start the rebuilding of the house. Holford's first steps in creating his arboretum, half a mile north-west of Westonbirt House, were taken in 1829, and three main avenues in the first layout of the arboretum are aligned on the house. He was particularly interested in north American conifers. Planting continued throughout the nineteenth century, and in the present century, directed by Sir George Lindsay Holford, and then by the 4th Earl of Morley. The arboretum has been owned by the Forestry Commission

Gilpin's great achievement is at Scotney Castle in Kent. Here Edward Hussey (1807–94) had Anthony Salvin design him a new house, which was built in 1837–43 some 300 yards above and to the north-east of the fourteenth-century fabric of Scotney Castle. Gilpin appears to have advised Hussey on the siting of his new house, and on the landscaping of the grounds. The decisive step was the retention of the more 'picturesque' elements of the old castle, leaving these as a dominant feature in the landscape. At the same time, it was decided to build a terraced 'bastion' near to the new mansion, to overlook the remains of the castle down in the lower grounds; and to exploit the rugged shapes of a quarry, between the new house and the old castle, by creating a woodland dell. In the course of the nineteenth century, the native woodland at Scotney was immensely enriched with new species, both trees – cypress, Lebanon cedar, Wellingtonia – and shrubs, such as rhododendron. Christopher Hussey (1899–1970) added immensely to the variety of the plantings after 1952.

As well as the general arboretum, Bicton had also a pinetum, begun in 1839, and an American Garden, 1840–3, which includes the Shell House of 1842, with a collection of shells and minerals – 'for the sake of those who are fond of these departments of science', as Loudon observed. In 1842, Loudon himself advised on the laying out of the long monkey puzzle avenue at Bicton – each tree was planted on a raised platform or mound. Though the property has been divided since 1957, these plantations largely survive in admirable maturity.

Described in one way or another many such arboreta or collections of trees were added to British gardens in the early nineteenth century. At Chatsworth, begun by Paxton in 1835, Loudon praises the arboretum in 1839 as 'the only one that we have seen or heard of, where sufficient room is given to every species to attain its usual size'. He comments also on the labelling of the trees – 'in white letters on a dark ground painted on heart of oak; but the letters are beginning to fade'. At Bicton, in 1842 – where the arboretum was begun around 1830 for Lord John Rolle – he admires

Left: The preservation of the old castle at Scotney, as a picturesque feature of the garden landscape, was William Sawrey Gilpin's master-stroke, when advising Edward Hussey in the 1830s. Within the forecourt of the castle is a small modern herb garden by Lanning Roper.

• • •

since 1956, and may now claim the most richly varied collection of trees in Britain.

W.S. Gilpin may have advised on the balustraded terrace added to the front of Nuneham Courtenay in 1832, and certainly devised the nine-acre pinetum laid out in the southern part. This has been taken over by the Oxford Botanic Garden, and enlarged to some 50 acres.

one great beauty . . . that every tree and shrub which it contains may be seen, and the name on its label read, by a person while sitting in a carriage, and driving through it along the green walk.

RARE AND EXOTIC SPECIES

Dunster Castle is a lesser yet beautiful example of such enthusiasm for rare trees. The old deer park was landscaped in the eighteenth century, and in the following century, the several terraces round the ancient castle, particularly the highest one, were planted with 'fine exotics'. Loudon noted

> a large lemon tree protected by glass during winter, a large pomegranate, large myrtles, passion flowers, wistarias, coronillas, and an immense hydrangea with both blue and pink flowers as a finale.

That was in 1842. In 1867 Anthony Salvin remodelled the castle, and added a conservatory, and in 1979, four years after the castle had been given to the National Trust, Graham Stuart Thomas admired the lemon tree, asking 'Is there another plant outside on our mainland? It is surely the ultimate in examples of the devotion of gardeners to the plants under their

care.' The gardens have been much restored by the National Trust.

Loudon wrote many pieces in his *Gardener's Magazine* in favour of these new and exciting woodland developments. At Highclere, he delights in 1833 that 'unfavourable circumstances of local climate' had 'induced His Lordship [Lord Carnarvon] to rely principally upon rhododendrons and azaleas for the decoration of his shrubberies', and of the walks at Christ Church and Magdalen, in Oxford, he says that their present state (1833) could be much improved by substituting new trees 'so as to form an arboretum'. In the same period extensive additions were made to the botanic collections at Syon Park, with advice from Richard Forrest, and linked with the construction of the Great Conservatory.

To my mind the most impressive of these collections of rare and exotic species is at Tresco, on the Isles of Scilly. Here in 1834 Augustus Smith began building his house, Tresco Abbey, and at the same time laying out

Left: The main north–south axis divides the long terraces of the gardens at Tresco, and leads to the Neptune figurehead, saved from the wreck of the SS Thames in 1841. While the plan may remind us of great Italian terrace gardens, like the Villa d'Este, the vegetation is astonishingly sub-tropical.

• • •

gardens beside the ruins of the old Priory, and along the terraces which he built on sloping ground to the west of his house. The main terrace walks were completed by 1855, and have the architectural form of the terraces at the Villa d'Este, with the possibility for the visitor to 'explore' to left or right as they ascend, or descend, the connecting stairs. But the planting is not Italian: it is sub-tropical. Smith had established shelter belts of holm oak, Monterey pine and Monterey cypress round his 17-acre gardens, and within this happy ground he set out areas of tender or half-hardy species which would, on the English mainland, survive only in sheltered or indeed enclosed sites. Augustus Smith died in 1872, by which time the gardens had been transformed, no less, from their earlier starkness, and the succeeding generations of the Dorrien-Smith family have continued the adventurous search for foreign plants which may be established at Tresco. Though plants are necessarily mixed, areas of concentration provide rich vistas of aeonium, or yucca, aloe, agave, echium – and what echium we can see at Tresco, growing up like Gaudi spires! – or

gazania. The steep areas close to the Abbey include the Mexico Garden, overlooked by a rocky wall and thick, or prickly, with succulents and cacti. Other regions offer rarities from South Africa or Australasia – protea, or bamboo, or tree ferns from New Zealand.

I have no doubt that a part of Tresco's glory rests on the firmly terraced plan, giving 'bones', a skeleton, to sustain the exuberance of the flora. Such a plan, with vistas and walks (though without the vital changes in level which Tresco enjoys), was imposed on the Brown landscape at Kew in the 1840s by Nesfield, when the Palm House was built by Burton and Turner. Round the Palm House Nesfield laid out a parterre, and he made the formal pool to the south-east (1847). His flower beds have mostly gone, but the vistas – like the Broad Walk – survive with the exuberant and astonishing growth of trees to either side. It was at this time – 1841 – that the gardens became a public research institute, with Sir William Hooker as the first Director, and their area was dramatically enlarged to some 240 acres. The Water Lily House, by Richard Turner, was added in 1852.

Right: *'Egypt' or the 'Egyptian Court' at Biddulph Grange. James Bateman's astonishingly varied gardens, comprising over a dozen distinct areas, are now in course of restoration by the National Trust. The tomb-like entrance here leads – to a Cheshire cottage!*

• • •

SECRET GARDENS

In a curious way the gardens at Biddulph Grange, made from scratch between the 1840s and the 1860s, contain a miniature version of the slowly developed marvels of Kew. James Bateman and his wife Maria, both dedicated botanists, began to lay out the many parts of their grounds in 1842, and were helped from 1849 onwards by their friend E.W. Cooke. Their combined knowledge of plants, architecture, mineralogy *and gardens* enabled them to create a closely knit yet brilliantly diverse group of garden scenes. Conservatories attached to the house allowed them a fernery and a camellia house; outside were Italianate terraces and parterres and the dahlia walk, with a long formal vista east to the deodar avenue. So far, we are formal indeed. But to south and south-east, the gardens embrace (yet divided each from each by rocky walls, hedges and barriers) a cosmopolitan mêlée of component parts. There is Egypt, with pairs of sphinxes before a sepulchral entrance (flanked by gigantic topiary

yew); the tunnel comes out in a Cheshire cottage; then there is the stumpery; and the pinetum; an arboretum; the quoit ground; the rhododendron ground; and *China*.

China, enclosed by high-piled ridges of rocks, and accessible only by a grotto tunnel or a well-concealed path through shrubbery, is carefully planned to be invisible from the rest of the gardens, and to be as convincingly 'Chinese' as the Batemans and Cooke could make it. The rocky ridge – the 'Great Wall' – has a Chinese watch tower, and the small lake is crossed by a red-lacquered Chinese bridge, and overlooked to one side by a Chinese pavilion. Thoughtfully chosen rocks rise from the lake, and all round its shores are exotic yet hardy species of Chinese or Far Eastern origin.

If 'China' at Biddulph is the most conscientiously concealed of any *giardino segreto* in this country, the 10-acre secret garden at Stancombe Park is quite as surprising, and has a spacious serenity all its own. The house, built in about 1840, has its own landscape views out over the valley and parkland, and its own gardens, which have been brilliantly developed since the mid-1960s. Far to one side a winding path leads to the valley and woodland beyond. Once in the wood, the path enters a tunnel, which leads past a cascade to the first surprise vista of the secret garden. This garden is wholly hidden by woodland from the house, a third of a mile away, and is so distant from the 'gardened' areas round the house that it is – like the Villa Farnese, deep in the woods at Caprarola – a wholly unexpected delight. Its history is slight, being supposedly made around 1850 by the Rev. David Edwards as a love-nest, discreetly distant from the house and his wife. I wonder. Certainly it is unexpected, and the opening views, as you emerge from the dark tunnel to the choice of rose-pergolas round each side of the lake, are enchanting. Beyond, the hillside rises up to a far-distant monument. Beside the lake, to one side, are more tunnels (curiously akin to Biddulph's 'Egypt' in style), and to the other a Doric temple is perched beside the lake, and overshadowed by gigantic copper beech and chestnut.

THE GREAT PLANT COLLECTIONS

The plant treasures of this country's gardens continued to be enriched throughout the nineteenth century, either with particular collections – at Bowood, the conifer collection was begun in 1848; the collection of rhododendrons in 1854 – or with more general collections of plants favoured by the local climate and terrain. At Abbotsbury, the undulating valley-ground, close to the Dorset coast, is further sheltered by thick plantations of holm oak. First in, and then beside an eighteenth-century walled garden, tender and sub-tropical plants were laid out by William Fox-Strangways, 4th Earl of Ilchester (1795–1865), and much increased later in the century. By 1899, over 5000 different plants were catalogued in the Abbotsbury gardens, and from the late 1960s energetic restoration followed by expansion of the gardens in the 1980s, to a total of some 20 acres, has led Allen Paterson to comment succinctly 'noteworthy specimens: too many to list'. Among the older plantings are camellias and Chusan palms, and an unmatched *Stranvaesia nussia*, which was planted in 1828, and named in honour of William Fox-Strangways – *Stranvaesia* being a Latinisation of his name. There is a later collection of hydrangea, another of eucalyptus,

and most recently a rose garden, a new region for Chinese plants and, in 1985, a conservatory designed to hold the national collection of *Salvia*.

Three other important collections of trees and shrubs were launched in the later nineteenth century – Sheffield Park, Leonardslee and Batsford Park. Capability Brown's landscaping of Sheffield Park in 1776 has already been mentioned. Something over a century later, the 3rd Earl of Sheffield brought in James Pulham (*c.* 1820–98) to enrich the lake-and-valley landscape with two more lakes, nearer to the house, linked by a waterfall, and with a smaller cascade joining them to Brown's lakes further down the valley. Pulham made a considerable name for himself in the mid- and later nineteenth century with his patented artificial rockwork – Pulhamite – which was installed for ferneries, rockeries, grottoes, cascades and the like in many gardens. The most famous examples were at Battersea Park, and at Sandringham. At Sheffield Park, Pulham's lake-

Below: 'And on a sudden, lo! the level lake' – the spacious yet deeply private 'secret garden' at Stancombe Park. Accessible from the house only by following a long, winding path, leading to a narrow tunnel, the secret garden was created in the 1850s.

· · ·

Right: *'A perfect treasure-house of rare plants!' – so wrote M.R. Gloag of the Abbotsbury gardens in 1906. By then, the original plantings of William Fox-Strangways, the 4th Earl of Ilchester, were in splendid maturity. The collections have been much enriched, and the gardens enlarged, in the later twentieth century.*

Opposite top: *Sir Edmund Loder's fine collection of rhododendrons and azaleas at Leonardslee was begun a century ago, progressively enriched with camellias, magnolias, maples, oaks and indeed conifers, to make it one of the most impressive woodland gardens in the country.*

Opposite bottom: *Bronze deer in the woodland at Batsford Park add to the oriental atmosphere of this part, planted with a great variety of maples, bamboos, flowering cherries and other Japanese or Chinese species. Nearby are the Japanese Rest House and a bronze Buddha.*

• • •

constructions were accompanied by varied plantings of conifers, such as Wellingtonia, swamp cypress and redwood, and also of Japanese maples. Between 1909 and 1934, these species were added to by a new owner, Arthur Gilstrap Soames, whose particular enthusiasm was for trees and shrubs having striking autumn colouring, and the overall development has been energetically continued since 1954, when the main area of woodland and lakes was purchased by the National Trust.

At Leonardslee, an area of 82 acres now holds one of the country's great collections of rhododendrons, azaleas, camellias and magnolias. It was laid out from 1889 onwards by Sir Edmund Loder, on the sides of a steep valley where many native trees were already growing, and where some fine Wellingtonia and redwood had been planted in the late 1850s. The house was built in 1855. Down the valley flows a stream, feeding a chain of pools – once used as hammer ponds – and there are superb views out over the Weald. As well as the main groups of species, there are also outstanding individual trees – a wonderful tulip tree, and an admirable incense cedar – and smaller garden areas such as the rock garden, with unusual plantings of small conifers.

The collection of trees at Batsford Park began in the 1890s, when the new mansion was completed in 1892 for A.B. Freeman-Mitford, later the 1st Lord Redesdale. His book *The Bamboo Garden* was published in 1896, and his central plantings at Batsford Park were of species from the Far East – bamboo, Japanese maple, flowering cherry, nutmeg – though many other species were included. The layout of the Japanese garden was given an additional Eastern flavour by means of architectural or sculptured features – a Japanese rest house, for example, and bronzes of deer. Lord Redesdale was at the same time an admirer of the garden theory of William Robinson, whose book *The Wild Garden* (1870) had also influenced Sir Edmund Loder at Leonardslee, in encouraging a natural and informal layout, where the old eighteenth-century respect for the 'genius of the place' – we might now say 'the lie of the land' – was coupled with a new interest in the characteristics (shape, colour, texture of bark and leaf) of the unnumbered species which had been introduced from abroad in the nineteenth century. The plantings at Batsford Park have been much extended since 1956, making a wide-ranging arboretum from the earlier more specialized collection.

Chapter Seven

ROMANTIC, BUT SEVERE

• • •

'*G*ardens should be romantic, but severe' wrote Vita Sackville-West in her long poem *The Garden* (1946). She goes on to insist that a garden *must* have a plan – or a framework – of paths, walls, hedges, where plants may then run riot. It is an epitome of her great creation at Sissinghurst. But her phrase covers the recurrent pushmepullyou of garden fashions ever since Eden. In this country, it has been centred on the formal (seventeenth-century) *versus* landscape (eighteenth-century) debate, but a lesser, splendid, comic and unresolved battle was waged 'about it and about' in the later nineteenth century.

On the formal side, the main polemicist was Sir Reginald Blomfield (1856–1942). His *The Formal Garden in England* (1892) was firmly architectural in its reference, and his supporters were for the most part garden designers with an architectural training. On the natural side, William Robinson (1839–1935) published several volumes to illustrate his theories – notably *The Wild Garden* (1870) and *The English Flower Garden* (1883) – which were generally supported by those more interested in plants than in the spaces where they were planted. As early as 1829 William Cobbett had written, in *The English Gardener*, distinguishing between flowers planted in *beds* ('a mass of one sort of flower') and in *borders*,

> where an infinite variety of them are mingled together, but arranged so that they may blend with one another in colour as well as in stature.

The gardens at Penshurst Place have been developed at many points in the last four centuries – not least since 1945. This Silver Garden, designed by John Codrington in the 1970s, provides quiet delight.

• • •

Above: 'It would be hard to find borders . . . in any way better done than those at Arley', wrote Gertrude Jekyll in 1904. By then, these borders had been laid out for over half a century – they are the oldest documented herbaceous borders in the country.

• • •

This – one of the first clear distinctions between massed bedding and the herbaceous border – was put into practice, in a tentative way, in several gardens in the early nineteenth century, often with the supposition that it was characteristic of early gardens of a 'Tudor', 'Elizabethan' or 'Shakespearian' kind. The best-authenticated example of an early herbaceous scheme is at Arley Hall, where in 1846 Rowland Egerton-Warburton and his wife Mary drew up a plan for the fine, 90-yard double borders, backed by a brick wall on one side, by a topiary yew hedge on the other. Since 1960 the gravel path between the borders has been replaced by turf, but in other respects the scheme has been faithfully maintained since its inception. George Elgood's painting of 1889, and Gertrude Jekyll's comments in their book *Some English Gardens* (1904) – 'throughout the length and breadth of England it would be hard to find borders of hardy flowers handsomer or in any way better done than those at Arley' – are still true today.

The herbaceous border, formed from groups of perennial flowers, sometimes with addition of shrubs, or of biennials, tends to be given a formal setting, backed against an architectural wall or topiary hedge. Yet its floral and leafy content is often endowed with an exuberance and irregularity of shape which contrasts (if well done!) superbly with the static containing lines of wall and path. It is this quality of abundance-within-order which makes the herbaceous bor-

der the triumphantly happy compromise between the formal and the natural in garden schemes. It puts flesh on the bones. They need each other.

THE FORMALISTS

Around 1891, Francis Inigo Thomas (a disciple of Blomfield) designed the main gardens at Athelhampton for A.C. de Lafontaine. By 2 September 1899, *Country Life* could praise Thomas's work as a brilliant resolution of the

> . . . feud, of that bitterness which appears to be inseparable from literary and artistic controversy between Mr. Robinson and those who think with him on the one hand, and a group of young and cultivated architects on the other.

The writer of the article, Avray Tipping, was, we may think, less than even-handed. The gardens at Athelhampton are wonderful – one of the marvels of the architectural style. Time has softened the stonework, so that it blends with that of the ancient hall, and the topiary yews in the Great Court have grown to a height of over 20 feet. Yet Thomas's garden areas – the Corona (*Country Life* calls it the 'Coronet'), the Great Court, with the Great Terrace above, and the Private Garden beyond the Corona, and to one side of the house – are brilliantly and undisguisedly architectural, enclosed or backed by walls, centred round stone-edged geometrical pools, and adorned with stone obelisks (the Corona) or obelisk-shaped topiary (the Great Court). The areas, at slightly different levels, are linked along connecting axes, divided yet joined by steps and gateways. And *planting* softens and enriches it all – now luxuriant, investing the walls, and with borders of shrubs and herbaceous plants. Further garden areas have been developed since the late 1950s, combining formal outlines, statuary and pools with a wide variety of planting. The White Garden leads northwards to the riverside walk along the bank of the Piddle. The Dry Garden, close to the Corona, has mainly sub-tropical plants and palms. Further to the east, beyond a rectangular canal made in 1969–70, is the walled kitchen garden. The nineteenth-century walls enclose geometrical areas, with a central pool and hedges of yew, beech and hornbeam.

Blomfield's most ambitious garden scheme is north of the border, at Mellerstain in Berwickshire. But several of his designs were laid out in England, at Chequers in the late 1890s (modified slightly by Avray Tipping around 1910), at Brocklesby after 1898, when he added a long, balustraded terrace to the south-east front, overlooking two geometrically shaped pools, one on each side of the main avenue; and at Godinton Park from 1902.

At Godinton the surrounding parkland is dotted with 'mature' trees – north of the house lies the bare trunk of an oak recorded in Domesday – but its history is scantily documented. The house itself has medieval fabric, remodelled in the seventeenth century, and then – crucial to our purpose – largely restored by Blomfield in 1902. At the same time he began the garden layout on three sides of the house, enclosing the several areas within clipped yew hedges to north, east and south. These hedges, laid out in 1902–6, are now like massive curving battlements, and serve both to shelter the gardens within, and to 'distance' the open grassland of the park from the house, rather in the manner of the early nineteenth-century balustraded terraces, yet with a vegetable rather than a mineral barrier.

Below: Green architecture – the noble topiary pyramids at Athelhampton were laid out, with most of the gardens, in 1891 or shortly afterwards. This spacious view of the Great Court is linked on the right with the Corona, the smaller, circular garden enclosed by walls in which are four gateways, each leading to a different garden area.

• • •

Below: A garden of steps, terraces, sculpture – and rural views. Iford Manor is famous for the garden Harold Peto created here in the early twentieth century. Like the larger and mainly level gardens at Hever Castle, it is enriched with many items of antique sculpture, but its essentially hillside site, necessitating many fine sets of steps, and woodland backing give it a character different from any other modern garden.

• • •

Within this great trimmed hedge, and set out on slightly sloping ground, is a topiary garden, formed with columns and pyramids of box, yew and cypress round the statue of Pan, looking southwards over the lawn, with herbaceous borders; beyond, on lower ground, and concealed by 'wings' of hedge, is the pool, a rectangle with curved ends, sunk well below the surrounding gardens, and partly shaded by weeping willow.

Round to the south-west, beyond an avenue of sorbus and flowering cherry, are lawns leading to the most brilliantly balanced garden features of any I know: *within*, backed against the walls of the kitchen garden, an Italian Garden, designed by Blomfield in 1916, and later modified – a small, private garden where the severity of the straight, central pool is relieved by abundant herbaceous bedding against the enclosing walls, and where the open colonnade and statues to the south look *out* on garden woodland – well-spaced and mature, the oak, cedar, copper beech, lime and chestnut are lavishly underplanted with bulbs and woodland

flowers. Again and again, we glimpse the countryside, over the battlemented hedge, or from a platform raised at the end of one of the paths.

'Romantic but severe' applies with joyous truth at Iford, a manor house in Wiltshire bought in 1899 by Harold Peto (1854–1933). He gardened here on his own account for thirty-odd years, firming up the (supposed) outlines of earlier terraces, furnishing these terraces with a multitude of sculptured pieces, laying lawns, and diversifying them and the backing woodland to the higher, north-eastern side of the terraces, with 'Italian' cypresses and flowering shrubs. Though the terraces may have been there in outline before he came, and though the woodland boasts some fine specimens – yew, cedar, beech, plane and chestnut – from the nineteenth century, the three-acre garden at Iford is really Peto's own.

Three main terraces, connected by flights of steps, rise up the hillside, behind and slightly to one side of the house. With varied views out over the valley of the Frome, seen from different

points and at different levels along the terraces, Iford is for me curiously reminiscent of William Kent's creation at Rousham, with a multiplicity of sculptural elements within the garden, and the continued awareness of peaceful country-side beyond. Yet had the Emperor Julian seen Iford (Horace Walpole had suggested that he might have chosen Rousham as his own), he would not have recognized all the sculpture. Along his terraces Peto assembled colonnades, broken or complete, a Spanish summerhouse, an octagonal garden house from the eighteenth century, and a medieval cloister, in and round which items are ranged from France, Germany, Byzantium and mainly from Italy. As at Rous-ham, there is a version of the dying Gaul. But, high on the hillside, there are traces of a Japanese garden, and steps leading to a column dedicated to 'Edward the Peacemaker' (Edward VII).

While the colonnades and sculpture at Iford may bring Rousham to mind, the main formal feature at Hever Castle, the Italian Garden, has strong echoes of the Villa Medici at Rome, as a luxurious open air setting for the choicest pieces of classical sculpture, often accompanied by colourful bedding. Walls and colonnades en-close a rectangular area of five acres, with alcoves and topiary subdivisions for particular 'exhibits'. To the east, an elaborate loggia (built 1908) looks out over the lake, created from the river Eden in 1904–8 by the firm of Joseph Cheal & Son to Frank Pearson's design, for William Waldorf Astor (created 1st Lord Astor in 1916). The Italian Garden is in fascinating contrast to the gardens round Hever Castle itself, restored for W.W. Astor in 1903–7, which have several areas of excellent topiary of a 'Tudor' kind beside the moat – a chess garden, a herb garden with sundial, and a maze. Many features have been restored or developed since 1970. South of the castle, the Golden Stairs rise up between informal plantings of azalea and rhododendron to the 500-yard terrace of Anne Boleyn's Walk, formed from the spoil from the lake. This terrace, well-planted with mature trees, has fine views over the different garden areas, and out to the southern parkland.

Above and below: The gardens at Hever Castle were laid out in the 1900s, with many varied features. William Waldorf Astor's main collection of classical sculpture is 'housed' in the 5-acre expanse of the Italian Garden, the south wall of which includes a number of grottoes.

• • •

GODINTON

$\bullet \quad \bullet \quad \bullet$

*T*he gardens of Godinton Park are the most important example in England of the work of Sir Reginald Blomfield. Known principally as an architect, his views on garden practice were none the less carefully elaborated, in *The Formal Garden in England*, published ten years before he began the remodelling of the house at Godinton, and laying out the surrounding gardens.

Though a little-known landscape designer, Sam Driver, is said to have worked in the old deer park at Godinton, Blomfield's layout of garden areas round the house appears to have been developed from scratch, constrained only by the kitchen block west of the house, and the walled kitchen gardens to the south-south-west. His yew hedges therefore enclosed the house on the remaining three sides – to north, east and south – taking in some twelve acres altogether.

Within these hedges, now sturdily dividing the gardens from the park, the different areas are separated by lesser hedges, and changes in level. To the south, the large, sunken Water Garden is admirably concealed from the main garden view, as is the small Italian Garden, which can be found round the corner to the west.

Top: *Three sides of the house at Godinton Park are enclosed by topiary hedges, laid out by Sir Reginald Blomfield in 1902–6 at the same time as his restoration of the old house. Round the house and gardens extends an ancient park and woodland (some 240 acres in all), with trees as old as any in England.*

Bottom left: *Blomfield's topiary schemes are a joyous vindication of his belief in control, order and balance within the garden. Here Pan plays thoughtfully to a distant nymph.*

Bottom centre: *Within the battlemented hedge, fine borders tell of modern delight in flowers Outside in the park, cattle graze peacefully.*

Bottom right: *The Italian Garden is a later part of Blomfield's scheme, and was modified by Mrs Bruce Ward in the 1920s. The cruciform pool leads the eye on to the loggia and statues at the end. Against the left-hand wall, the summerhouse gives a way into the kitchen garden.*

• • •

Right: To east and west
of the Great Plat at
Hestercombe, the raised
terraces carry long
stone-edged 'rills' set in
lawns between borders.

• • •

THE 'NATURAL' GARDENERS

Against these formal schemes – or, more accurately, against their cruder manifestations – arose the opposition, violent and entertaining, of William Robinson, in books and articles, many in his own periodical *The Garden*, founded in 1871. Carpet bedding, topiary, pergolas, formal pools, and rigid outlines, whether of grand designs or of the lesser shapes of paths or flower beds, all were attacked; and in their place he advocated the subtle beauty of wild flowers grown casually, and of *any* plants and flowers, including the latest exotics imported from remotest lands, grown with respect for the 'natural form and beauty of the plants'. His own garden and surrounding woodland at Gravetye Manor in West Sussex (acquired by Robinson in 1885) exemplified 'natural' or 'wild' gardening for many years, but a promi-

nent terraced area near the house was in fact laid out in geometrical beds.

Robinson's ideas found much support with Miss Gertrude Jekyll (1843–1932), who first met him in 1875. In the 1860s she had been an art student at the Kensington School of Art, and was much influenced by the water-colourist Hercules Brabazon, and by his theories and by those of later Impressionists to do with light, and the relationships of colours, which she carried over, with supreme success, to the domain of plant and flower arrangement in the garden. In addition to her long connection with Robinson, she met in 1889 the young architect Edwin (later Sir Edwin) Lutyens (1869–1944) with whom she collaborated on many house-and-garden schemes. Her numerous and influential books on garden design and planting include *Wood and Garden*, 1899; *Home and Garden*, 1900, and *Colour in the Flower Garden*,

1908. Among the earliest instances of her work with Lutyens was the development of her own property at Munstead Wood, where Lutyens built the house in 1895–7, and she created the gardens. The original area of some 15 acres has been reduced to 10, and some garden features have been drastically modified since the 1950s, following division of the property.

The gardens at Munstead Wood were divided into separate areas, with strikingly different characters, flowering seasons and purposes. The north court, shaded by the gallery of the house, is quiet and secluded; nearby is a nut walk leading to a pergola; beyond was the main flower border, and then (to the north-west) the kitchen garden, divided into practical plots and bright with flower borders. To the south and south-east the areas were more 'natural', with walks through woodland, each with a separate identity derived from the enclosing trees and

underplanting. Though much of the detail of her creation has gone, her plans and planting schemes survive (see, for example, Chapter 2 of J. Brown's *Gardens of a Golden Afternoon*). In 1906, in *A Book of English Gardens*, M.R. Gloag could already write of Jekyll's outstanding *artistic* success:

> This Garden belongs to an artist in the highest sense of the word . . . Every moment leads to the discovery of a new colour effect or audacious colour contrast . . . as carefully planted with flowers as a painter arranges colour on his canvas; 'not dropped down in lifeless dabs as he has them on the palette,' but placed with 'forethought and deliberation'.

If many parts of the Munstead Wood scheme were laid out in a 'natural' style (of a sort Robinson would have approved), the collaboration of Jekyll and Lutyens led more often to gardens with an instantly evident *architectural* framework, in which Jekyll's flower and shrub planting could flow, or spill over, in painterly abundance. At Mells Manor House – mentioned in Chapter One for the outstanding sixteenth-century garden walls – Lutyens and Jekyll created a scheme of hedged lawns, using a part of the old framework, and a terrace with loggia facing a formal, rectangular bedding scheme. This was in 1901 or 1902. In 1904 or shortly after, they worked together at Hestercombe, continuing at intervals until 1910.

At Hestercombe, an extensive landscape with temples and cascade had been made in the mid- and later eighteenth century by the artist C.W. Bampfylde, who was a friend of Henry Hoare at Stourhead. Most of his work is now concealed in forestry development, but the four acres of formal gardens made by Lutyens and Jekyll survive as the finest example of their joint labours, and enjoying magnificent views over the countryside. Below, and south of the house (which he did not design), Lutyens laid out the Great Plat, a magnificent sunken garden quadrangle, enclosed to east and west by raised terraces, each carrying a long 'rill' of water in a formal channel, and enclosed to the south by one of his grandest pergolas. Yet – being essentially an 'open' structure – it does not fully enclose the scene, allowing the eye to view the further landscape. The Great Plat itself is crossed by diagonals of lawn, and the four triangles, one along each side, are filled with stone-edged beds and borders.

HESTERCOMBE

· · ·

*A*fter much sniping at the Victorian remodelling of the mansion at Hestercombe, Lawrence Weaver turned with delight to Lutyens' work in the gardens: 'the orangery, the rotunda and the retaining walls at the head of the two water-terraces. The first thing that strikes us about these is that they undoubtedly possess style.' This 'style', he points out, is related to a deep understanding of *garden* architecture, particularly that of the Renaissance and the period of Louis XIV, and a conscious gradation from the smoothly finished masonry of the inner parts of the garden to the rough, dry-stone structures on the boundaries – 'as the orangery is the most polished piece of building in the gardens, so is the outside walling of the main terraced garden the most rugged and simple . . . It is the last outwork of man on the edge of Nature.'

Hestercombe was created by Lutyens and Jekyll between 1904 and 1910, and is an outstanding example of their long and fruitful partnership. Since 1973 the gardens have been scrupulously restored, and Gertrude Jekyll's original plantings have been carefully re-established, giving superb – but gentle – flesh to Lutyens' framework.

Above: *A domed circular pool set in a wall was one of Lutyens' favourite motifs. This lily pool, grown round with vine and acanthus, marks the beginning of the East Water Garden.*

Left: *The Great Plat at Hestercombe is technically a sunken garden, since it has raised walks or terraces on all four sides, and is reached from each corner by a flight of steps (in characteristic Lutyens style). But its spacious dimensions, and the airy nature of the pergola, always allow a sense of connection with the outside landscape, stretching far away to the south.*

Far left: *An open yet architectural feature, Lutyens' great pergola runs for 75 yards along the south side of the Great Plat, enclosing its formal scheme with a superb combination of control – the repeated regularity of pillars and cross-beams – and abundance in planting. Lavender below, roses and clematis climbing up and over the framework.*

• • •

Right: The main east–west vista at Hidcote – the top of the T-shaped framework. This vista includes the Red Borders, in the foreground; the twin summerhouses (at this point, to the left, the long stem of the 'T' begins); the clipped lime avenue, and last the wrought-iron gates, giving on to the ha-ha and rural view.

• • •

The north-east corner of the Great Plat leads up to the paved, open Rotunda, with a central pool. From this point you may gaze either south, along the eastern rill, or eastwards to the other main area of the gardens: the 100-yard long rectangular layout for the Orangery, and the Dutch Garden beyond. This area is rich with steps and balustrades – down, in stages, to the Orangery and its long terrace, and up again to the Dutch Garden. In 1925, Lawrence Weaver wrote rapturously of Lutyens' achievement:

He has weighed the full possibilities of the site, the peculiar character of local materials and the manifold methods of modern gardening, and he has brought to the design invention and ingenuity, imagination and learning. That is why it has style. It is the work of a particular man in a particular place.

Today, after extensive restoration of the gardens by Somerset County Council since 1973, it is fairer to say 'they' rather than 'he'. Jekyll's planting has been restored in large part, with striking drifts of bergenias and white lilies in the main borders; and in the Dutch Garden grey foliage beds, with yuccas and roses.

GERTRUDE JEKYLL

It is, I suspect, a Jekyll-and-Lutyens *style*, built up in the public mind from many gardens, many books and many illustrations, particularly the gentle flood of water-colours produced by George Elgood, Katharine Wyatt, Beatrice Parsons, E.A. Rowe, Henry Sage and others between 1890 and 1920, which has since been so much admired, and so influential, rather than an individual garden. Yet in the period of their most fruitful collaboration, two particular gardens, Hidcote (begun *c.* 1908) and Great Dixter (begun 1911) provided specific inspiration for the *design* of numerous later gardens, with which Jekyll's sensitive understanding of plants – colours, textures, forms *and* growing patterns – could be combined.

Hidcote Manor in Gloucestershire was bought by the American Major Lawrence Johnston in 1907, and the gardens – ten acres, begun from scratch – were developed from the following year until 1948, when he gave the property to the National Trust. His particular achievement was to unite his grounds with two main vistas or axes – exactly like a 'T' in shape – each largely enclosed by hedges of yew, beech or lime; and to site many different garden areas, likewise separated to a greater or lesser extent by hedges, in the regions to the left (west) and right (east) of the 'stem' of the T. This provided a strong sense of an overall plan, together with the possibility of developing the smaller sections of the gardens in distinctive ways. Obviously, the idea of having different, and possibly contrasting, areas in one's garden is as old as the wish for variety itself; but Lawrence Johnston's interest in creating a succession of 'garden rooms', as these separated areas have come to be called, was not to facilitate different architectural features, or even to allow wide variation in elements of garden design, but principally to allow the greatest variety in the *planting* of each area – in terms of seasonal interest, or colour schemes or, to some extent, in terms of 'formal' or 'natural' design.

While there are two important outward views at Hidcote – from the left-hand side of the top of the T, looking to the west, and south from the bottom of the 'stem' – most of the garden areas are self-contained, but with appealing glimpses through the hedges into neighbouring 'rooms'. The eastern and western areas begin with ground sloping down southwards, and divided into formal and strongly architectural sections, achieved by enclosing topiary, by marked patterns of brickwork and paving, and (to the west) by terracing and by a sequence of tall topiary 'pillars'. On each side, further to the south, the planting is much less formal – to the south-east, a series of glade and woodland scenes, and to the south-west, a stream garden of a 'wild' character.

Though I have explained the device of 'garden rooms' at some length, their excitement at Hidcote comes above all from their rich and thoughtful planting. Vita Sackville-West said of this

> What I should like to impress upon the reader is the luxuriance everywhere; a kind of haphazard luxuriance, which of ·course comes neither by hap nor by hazard at all.

The hedges are varied – holm oaks, different hollies, box, hornbeam, copper beech – and the planting within them is wonderful: the 'Red Borders', and roses; and the fuchsia garden; paeonies; areas of autumn berries and colourful leaves in the woodland garden; and 'Hidcote' lavender – of course.

Since 1948, Hidcote has no longer been guided onwards by Lawrence Johnston; but the fortunes of Great Dixter have been in the hands of the Lloyd family ever since the property was acquired by Nathaniel Lloyd in 1910, and the five acres of gardens were designed, principally by Lutyens, in 1911. To Lutyens' plan (dated July 1911) Nathaniel Lloyd added his own design for the Sunken Garden in 1923. Following the death of Nathaniel Lloyd, the gardens were further developed by Mrs Daisy Lloyd, and then by their son Christopher Lloyd, who has increased Dixter's fame both by his long and successful development of the gardens, and by his fine books on gardening and particularly on his own work at Great Dixter. We might note,

among others, *The Mixed Border* (1957, 1985); *The Well-Tempered Garden* (1970, 1985) and *The Year at Great Dixter* (1987).

Like Hidcote, the garden at Great Dixter is brilliantly divided into separate yet connected areas – but with more than one difference. At Hidcote, the house – Hidcote Manor – is one of the least important elements in the garden, visible only in some of the eastern areas. At Great Dixter, the garden areas are all, from one angle or another, related to the house, whose tiled and half-timbered outlines are close in the viewer's mind at every point in the tour of the gardens. The house – fifteenth-century, with a sixteenth-century wing imported by Lutyens – stands central in the gardens, and their divisions and their character are occasionally achieved by Lutyens' architecture in brick. This applies, for example, to the archways and steps dividing the Sunken Garden, the Walled Garden and the lawn round the western side of the house. At most other points, however, the divisions are achieved by hedges of clipped yew, which, in company with the mature and joyous topiary figures (mainly in the south-western lawn, and in the enclosed area to the north-east of the house) give a recurrent tone to the different parts of the garden.

Below: Peacocks in animated colloquy – and trimmed to perfection. The topiary courtyard to the east of the house at Great Dixter.

• • •

SISSINGHURST

• • •

*F*or many garden lovers, Sissinghurst represents the high point of twentieth-century garden achievement, with profuse, varied and subtle planting of flowers and shrubs in an equally subtle layout of 'garden rooms', separated from each other by clipped hedges and ancient walls, yet connected by intriguingly varied 'doorways' and passages.

The property was acquired in 1930, and developed until the 1940s by Vita Sackville-West and her husband Sir Harold Nicolson. While he is credited with the general plan, the planting schemes were the creation of Vita Sackville-West, and have been scrupulously maintained since her death in 1962.

The tall Tower, built by Sir Richard Baker in the 1560s, rises high up above the layout of different garden areas, and gives wonderful, rarely equalled views down into the Rondel, the Cottage Garden, the Tower Courtyard, the Tower Lawn and the White Garden, and further out to the Orchard, the Nuttery and the Moat Walk, and to the countryside beyond. Like the Tower itself, and many of the garden walls, the Moat Walk is a reminder of the late-medieval origins of Sissinghurst Castle. The sunken Moat Walk is dry, grassed over and planted on one side with azaleas, but two 'arms' of water-filled moat survive, dating from the early 1500s or before.

Above: The White Garden, in one of its 'whitest' moments. This part of the gardens was laid out in 1946 – virtually the last area to be created – and the iron canopy was added in 1972. In the background is the sixteenth-century tower.

Left: 'The lavish best' at Sissinghurst. Abundance and extravagance of roses in the firm framework of clipped hedges and paved walks.

Far left: Geometrical, yet subtly asymmetrical – a characteristic of many garden areas at Sissinghurst. Here each of the paths is straight, but one is set at a slight angle to the other. Gaps in the hedges (indicating further delights to discover) are hinted at by the bands of light on the paving stones.

• • •

Within each of these areas, the planting and the atmosphere are vitally different. Between the front gate and the house are lawns, planted as a flowery meadow of rich and welcome beauty in the spring; the paved Sunken Garden (with a central pool) is ringed with diverse climbing plants, clematis and vines; and the Rose Garden, to the south-west, is enclosed by massive buttresses of yew. The main south lawn is overlooked from the north by the house, by Lutyens' great terrace and by one of the very best surviving examples of Lutyens' clover-leaf step designs. The lawn is scattered with orchard trees, and southwards there is a pond, the vestige of an earlier moat.

For many today the supreme feature at Great Dixter is the Long Border, east of the terrace and steps. For some seventy yards, this broad border spreads its glory from east to west. It was at first purely a herbaceous border, but has evolved gradually to contain a mixture of shrubs and herbaceous and other perennial plants. Apart from its long period of summer beauty, its *mixed* character allows it solidity and dignity even in the bleakest moments of winter.

GARDEN ROOMS AT SISSINGHURST

Obliquely and directly, both Great Dixter and Hidcote influenced Sissinghurst, the most important garden in England in this century. Vita Sackville-West, who bought the (virtually derelict) property of Sissinghurst Castle in 1930, had earlier cut her teeth in garden matters at Long Barn, near Sevenoaks in Kent, where she and her husband Sir Harold Nicolson had lived from 1915 to 1930. There, their plans had been slightly modified by Lutyens in 1925, and it would be foolish to suggest that she and Sir Harold had not also been influenced in their ideas of garden design, planting and plant associations by Gertrude Jekyll.

In the easy, loosely-rhyming lines of her long poem, *The Garden*, Vita Sackville-West pours out her fascination with the tasks, challenges and rewards of gardening, particularly at Sissinghurst, through the four seasons. In 'Summer', she writes with a voice of understanding and authority of the absolute need for each and every garden to have a *plan*, to have a firm structure in and round and over which the

Right: Christopher Lloyd's dachshund Tulipa inspects the Long Border at Great Dixter. Even in winter, this mixed border remains interesting, and immensely attractive, with areas of evergreen foliage and striking forms of twig and branch.

• • •

exuberance of loved plants may thrive. The gardener's work of *pruning* is to reassert the original plan – 'design his object', she writes; and if the plan is good, and firm, then the planting can be as 'wild' as one likes:

> Gardens should be romantic, but severe.
> Strike your strong lines, and take no
> further care
> Of such extravagance as pours the rose
> In wind-blown fountains down the
> broken walls,
> In gouts of blood, in dripping flower-falls,
> Or flings the jasmine where the walls
> enclose
> Separate garths, a miniature surprise.

By 1946, when *The Garden* appeared in print, the creation of Sissinghurst was virtually complete. It is a commonplace to say that in this creation, Sir Harold Nicolson was principally involved in the design, and Vita Sackville-West was responsible for the planting. Certainly there are 'strong lines' in the design, and it is abundantly sure that these are clothed with an 'extravagance' of flowers. Though the mainly sixteenth-century buildings at Sissinghurst were near to derelict in 1930, many stretches of wall remained to provide the 'strong lines' of distinct garden areas, as you may see at once, when entering the first garden courtyard, or in breathtaking panorama from the top of the high Tower, which rises up in the near-centre of the gardens.

The steep, downward views from the Tower are a rare and special quality of these gardens. From this high point, you can see down into almost every point of the ten-acre gardens (and see how each area is distinct, divided from those around by walls or hedges), and you can see the Kentish countryside, of farm and woodland, round about. And you can see – if you look closely – that, though the enclosures, or sections, or 'garden rooms' are mostly square or rectangular in shape, the straight paths which run through them are often slightly *slanted* at the point where they pass from one area to another. This characteristic (due, in part, to the slightly asymmetrical layout of the sixteenth-century walls) adds a most special and entrancing quality to the gardens, since, again and again, the *far end* of a path or vista stretching through several 'garden rooms' is not immediately visible. You, the visitor, are therefore tempted to walk onwards through the gardens to explore, to discover what statue or what

viewpoint lies at the end; and as you advance, you are continually tempted by other choices, other prospects of floral delight which you glimpse through doorways, through gaps in the wall or hedge, or even through window-spaces in the now roofless walls.

While some areas, like the Rose Garden and the Rondel, or the White Garden, have a geometrical framework which is apparent at once (though the profusion of white roses in the White Garden may so seize our attention that the 'design' is forgotten), others, like the old orchard, or the Nuttery, underplanted with abundance of primroses and polyanthus, are deliberately 'natural' in their presentation. This 'naturalness' is achieved only with unremitting care. At Sissinghurst, the continuity of planting has been unbroken since the 1930s. The National Trust, who have owned the property since 1967, may be justly proud of their record here, maintaining the gardens in impeccable order, while allowing an ever-growing multitude of visitors to enjoy them.

Above: The rondel seen from Sissinghurst's tower, with Kentish countryside beyond.

• • •

NEW FOR OLD

Between 1908, when Lawrence Johnston began work on the gardens at Hidcote, and the mid-twentieth century, when the layout of the

Above: The Savill Garden, set within the eastern confines of Windsor Great Park, was developed from 1932 onwards by Sir Eric Savill as a 'natural' setting for all kinds of hardy trees and plants, and with a special interest in water-loving species.

• • •

gardens at Sissinghurst was completed, many other English parks and gardens were developed, either from scratch, or by additions or alterations to older schemes. The Arboretum at Westonbirt, begun in the early nineteenth century, was extended by Sir George Holford in the early twentieth century, and from 1956 onwards, when the Forestry Commission became owners of the Arboretum, several additional plantations were added, so that the total area is now around 360 acres. On the eastern side of Windsor Great Park, another garden concerned with 'plants' rather than 'plan' – and, we might think, the most important and successful example of the 'wild garden' propounded by William Robinson – was established in 1932 by Sir Eric Savill. First named the Bog Garden, as it was essentially a moist and in parts watery woodland area, it was named the Savill Garden by King George VI in 1951. Extended in the early 1950s, and again in 1977, its area is now some 34 acres, and the original area of woodland, ponds and stream has come to include both an exhilarating diversity of trees and shrubs among the original woodland species of oak and beech, alternating with grassy glades, and areas of a more formal kind. These now include a group of raised alpine beds, a rose collection and herbaceous borders. To my mind, the most beautiful of the Savill Garden's delights is the broad carpet of moss, overshadowed by beech trees near the Upper Pond,

which is Europe's 'sincerest form of flattery' in relation to the perfect moss garden, Koke-dera, within the Saiho-ji Temple garden at Kyoto in Japan.

Delight in particular plants has again been shown at St Paul's Walden Bury, where since 1932, to the west of the house and the central lawn, fine flower gardens and a rhododendron garden have been created by Sir David Bowes Lyon (who was President of the Royal Horticultural Society) and Simon Bowes Lyon. At Hardwick Hall, one quarter of the original garden area has been redeveloped as England's most gorgeous herb garden. Designed by Paul Miles in the early 1970s, it is of a Renaissance richness and exuberance (see the central pyramids of golden hops) which makes you forget that the plants are nearly all intended for medicine or the pot – for flavour, for savour, for medicine, and even 'for weakness of the brain', a problem which I understand.

Often enough in the twentieth century the elaborate – and costly – garden schemes of older days have been simplified, or even totally destroyed, reduced to lawn and tennis courts. In memorable and exceptional gardens, however, this has not happened, and the challenging existence of Victorian schemes has occasionally led to the creation of equally interesting modern gardens. This has happened at Longleat, where the formal displays of massed bedding between the house and the orangery were replaced in the

Left: The gardens of many Oxford and Cambridge colleges are renowned for the excellence of their herbaceous borders. At Cambridge, the Fellows' Garden of Clare College was laid out in its present form by Walter Barlow in 1946–7, to the design of Professor Willmer.

• • •

1940s by a simpler, yet consciously formal and dignified layout designed by Russell Page.

'AN INFINITE VARIETY': THE HERBACEOUS BORDER

Already in 1904 Gertrude Jekyll had commented on the 'box edgings' of the parterre at Penshurst Place that they had 'in themselves an air of solidity and importance that befits the large scale of the place'. She referred to George Devey's reconstruction of the great parterre, undertaken around 1850, and further developed by Lord de L'Isle in the 1890s. Lord de L'Isle had also established splendid herbaceous borders in the 11-acre walled gardens, which she acknowledged with the phrase, 'Herbaceous plants are grandly grown throughout this beautiful garden'. Her words may indeed be truer today than in 1904, since the gardens have been keenly and originally reshaped since 1945 by the present Lord de L'Isle. Garden designers have been engaged such as Lanning Roper (for a double border, with foliage plants and shrubs) and John Codrington (for the Silver Garden), and Lord de L'Isle has himself recently created the colourful garden with a Union Jack pattern in roses and lavender, beside which is a small 'mount' or viewing platform, on whose slopes are the national emblems, set out in box.

These modern developments at Penshurst Place have a special atmosphere, for they are nearly all placed in a context of orchard trees, old, full of individual character, yet in disciplined patterns like the quincunx of the plantings in the hunting parks of Persian kings. Old-and-yet-new, 'romantic yet severe' applies to perfection at Penshurst.

Jekyll would praise the varied borders at Penshurst today as highly as those she admired in 1904. I do not know if she saw the walled gardens at Helmingham Hall – they were certainly recorded in water-colours by E. Arthur Rowe in 1892, and again in photographs in the second volume of Charles Holme's *Gardens of England* in 1908. In the 1980s, the herbaceous borders at Helmingham may claim to be the equals of any in England, and their splendour is matched by the quiet yet seductive beauty of the vegetables and espaliered fruit trees on either side.

England is rich in herbaceous borders, and visitors from abroad may be forgiven if they think that we have had them since the year dot. We haven't, and their gorgeous yet calculated month-after-month display is not much more than a century old in its invention. In the age-old setting of Oxford or Cambridge colleges, it is easy, therefore, to be deceived by the architecture, from the time of Elizabeth, or Charles I. Round these venerable buildings, the floral displays are – relatively – new. I have already written about Capability Brown's plan to 'landscape' the Backs at Cambridge. Among the

Below: Herbaceous borders on a heroic scale at Newby Hall. They extend for some 300 yards between the house and the banks of the river Ure, and were created from 1925.

• • •

colleges which his scheme would have affected is Clare College, and today the Fellows' Garden at Clare may boast as splendid and thoughtfully conceived herbaceous borders as any in Cambridge or Oxford (there are close rivals in Emmanuel and Trinity Hall, in Cambridge, and at St John's at Oxford. But the league table is not static.) The borders in the Fellows' Garden at Clare were laid out in 1946–7 – in a garden

area which had existed, with lawn and fruit trees, since 1688.

Borders of greater length, and as much magnificence, extend southwards from Newby Hall along the main axis of the gardens, towards the river Ure. Here we have, as Arthur Hellyer said, 'an old house with a new garden'. Celia Fiennes had already written in the 1690s, 'this was the finest house I saw in Yorkshire'. The

present borders at Newby Hall are over 300 yards in length – I know no longer – with yew hedges on either side. They were *created* (and here the word deserves a fuller emphasis, which italics cannot convey) by Major Edward Compton from 1925 onwards. His work at Newby Hall involved many other garden features on either side of the great axial borders, incorporating elements of the earlier framework.

Heale House in Wiltshire has a similar mixture of old and new. While the house – built in the seventeenth century and enlarged after 1894 by Detmar Blow – has early garden elements to the west designed by Harold Peto from 1906, the eighteenth-century walled kitchen garden to the south-west was not developed until the 1970s. The southern wall has been replaced by a pergola, and the central planting – still related to a foursquare division of the most traditional kind – is a delicious mixture of the lovely and the worthwhile. Horace wrote of this, long ago, 'qui miscuit utile dulci'. At Heale there is also a Japanese garden, created in 1901.

HISTORICAL RECONSTRUCTIONS

Near the beginning of this book, I pointed out that the gardens of the Middle Ages and of the Renaissance in this country exist only as 'frameworks', as 'skeletons', with walls of cloisters and quadrangles, with terraces and garden buildings surviving, but no longer having the *planting* which was there originally. Reconstructions or recreations of these vanished gardens, or some of their features, have been attempted since the mid-nineteenth century, as I have already said, and nowhere more successfully than at Hatfield. Here the framework of gardens laid out in the early seventeenth century for the 1st Earl of Salisbury suffered greatly from 'landscaping', but from the early nineteenth century onwards successive restorations have been undertaken, culminating in the work of the present Marchioness of Salisbury. While the Great Maze, established in 1841 below the terrace and upper garden on the east side of Hatfield House, is the most striking of the nineteenth-century

Above: Apple trees trained over a metal framework form a green tunnel along this axis of the walled kitchen garden at Heale House. This garden area, with eighteenth-century walls, has been memorably developed since the 1970s as a mixed garden of fruit, vegetables, flowers and ornamental climbers.

• • •

features, the pattern and planting of both the east garden as a whole, and the upper west garden have been redesigned and enriched in the 1970s. The most intriguing historical reconstruction is also the most recent – the sunken knot garden created in 1980–1 to the north-west of Hatfield House, beside the east front of the Old Palace. This garden is planted with flowers, herbs and shrubs appropriate to the period of the design (including many which would have been known to, and even introduced by, John Tradescant). One quarter of the garden is designed as a low, box-hedged labyrinth.

There has been an upsurge of interest in mazes in recent years, and many have been laid out, sometimes in bizarre patterns and with unusual materials. A fine hedge-maze with polygonal outline has been planted in 1976 at Port Eliot – it can be glimpsed, in the eastern part of the gardens, from Brunel's railway viaduct. The viaduct itself, built in the 1850s, forms a spectacular 'eye-catcher' seen from the gardens.

At Chatsworth, where the gardens have evolved continuously since their inception in the sixteenth century, another maze has been created, in the 1970s, on the site of a vanished nineteenth-century marvel, Paxton's Great Stove. This huge conservatory was demolished in 1920, and the maze has been laid out within the rectangular area of its surviving foundation walls. In 1970, a new conservatory, of strikingly modern design, was built nearer to Paxton's surviving Conservative Wall.

Left: This knot garden at Hatfield House has been created since 1980, incorporating patterns from sixteenth-century garden manuals, and many plants from that period. It replaces a rose garden laid out around 1875, and is overlooked by the Old Palace, built in the 1480s. The knot garden is characteristic of the imaginative development of the gardens at Hatfield in recent years.

Below: The thirteen arches of Isambard Kingdom Brunel's railway viaduct cross the river Tiddy near to the south-east corner of the park and gardens at Port Eliot, forming a gigantic nineteenth-century 'eye-catcher'. The eighteenth-century parkland is complemented by gardens, with fine areas of azaleas and rhododendrons – and a modern maze.

• • •

Above: The topiary at Hall Place, Bexley, is among the finest in Britain – and relatively modern, having been largely developed since the late 1960s. These abstract figures are accompanied by the joyous line of the 'Teddy Bears' picnic', of which the first participant appears on the far right.

• • •

'A FLOWERY GARDEN PLACE'

I finish this survey of the fine historic parks and gardens of England with two recent creations, which between them contain most admirable examples of what is *formal* and of what is *natural* in garden design and planting. Hall Place, in Bexley, was built in the fifteenth and sixteenth centuries, but little is known of its garden history before the 1890s, when formal bedding to the north and a few clipped yews in the terraced lawns to the west are recorded. Many mature trees date from this period. Then in 1969 the property was taken over by the London Borough of Bexley, and the grounds – some 62 acres – became a public park. Round the house several garden areas were developed, set in the earlier framework of walls and terraces, and bounded by the river Cray to the south. There is a rose garden, a herb garden, areas of herbaceous borders, another of formal bedding; and above all, there is topiary. Some is abstract in shape, and striking enough, seen against the flint-studded walls of the old house – but the line of a dozen or so bears, eight to ten feet tall, laughing and gesturing, sticking their clipped yew stomachs out, this 'Teddy Bears' picnic' is a masterpiece, and not unworthy of comparison with the topiary at Levens Hall.

The garden of East Lambrook Manor in Somerset is the smallest to be described in this book – it is just over one acre in size – yet it is amazingly rich with plant delight, and all created since 1939. In that year, Walter and Marjorie Fish bought the property, and began to plan their gardening. In her principal book on East Lambrook Manor, *We Made a Garden* (1956, 1983) Marjorie Fish wrote

> You can't make a garden in a hurry . . . House and garden must look as if they had grown up together . . . We didn't start work outside for nearly a year.

But once started, their work was dedicated – if not always unanimous. She writes amusingly about her stratagems to outwit her husband's less adventurous policies – particularly her wish to get rid of a series of roses on poles, and replace them with a double row of dwarf cypress. She won – the roses were banished to the boundary walls, and the long 'avenue' of clipped *Chamaecyparis lawsoniana* still gives solidity and order beside her exciting and irrepressible underplanting. Indeed, 'solidity' and 'order' are essential beneath the liberality of plants – she herself wrote that she agreed entirely with her husband's dictum that 'the four essentials of a good garden are perfect lawns, paths, hedges and walls'. These, the 'framework', were well-established at East Lambrook Manor before his death in 1947. Marjorie Fish continued to garden, to enrich and diversify the planting, and to write well and clearly about it until her death in 1969.

Since then, different owners have continued, and slightly varied the composition. This is as it should be, for no garden can, or should stand still. The wealth of primroses, nearly lost a few years ago, has been restored, and the framework of walls, slight terraces and paths has again been loaded with crane's-bill, aquilegia, fritillaries, dianthus and hellebore. The garden is reminiscent of Thomas Campion's praise of his mistress' face:

> It is a flowery garden place
> Where knots of beauties have such grace
> That all is work and nowhere space.

Below: Do not be deceived. The profusion – and beauty – of the planting at East Lambrook Manor rests on a garden plan as firm as anyone could wish. Exuberance is based, triumphantly, on order.

• • •

A GUIDE TO ENGLAND'S GRADE 1 GARDENS

· · ·

NORTHUMBERLAND
1. Alnwick Castle, *Alnwick*
2. Belsay Hall, *Belsay*

CUMBRIA
3. Levens Hall, *Levens, Kendal*

NORTH YORKSHIRE
4. Castle Howard, *Henderskelf*
5. Duncombe Park, *Helmsley*
6. Hackfall, *Grewelthorpe*
7. Rievaulx Terrace, *Ryedale*
8. Studley Royal, *Harrogate*

WEST YORKSHIRE
9. Bramham Park, *Wetherby, Leeds*
10. Harewood House, *Leeds*

SOUTH YORKSHIRE
11. Wentworth Castle, *Stainborough*

HUMBERSIDE
12. Sledmere House, *Driffield*

MERSEYSIDE
13. Birkenhead Park, *Wirral*

WEST MIDLANDS

STAFFORDSHIRE
27. Alton Towers, *Farley*
28. Biddulph Grange, *Biddulph*
29. Shugborough Hall, *Colwich*

SHROPSHIRE
30. Hawkstone Park, *Hodnet*

WARWICKSHIRE
31. Compton Verney, *Stratford on Avon*
32. Farnborough Hall, *Banbury*
33. Packwood House, *Lapworth*
34. Warwick Castle, *Warwick*

NORTHAMPTONSHIRE
35. Althorp, *Daventry*
36. Boughton House, *Weekley, Kettering*
37. Castle Ashby, *Northampton*
38. Drayton House, *Lowick*

HEREFORD & WORCESTER
39. Croome Court, *Great Malvern*

NORFOLK
40. Holkham Hall, *Fakenham*

OXFORDSHIRE
104. Christ Church, *Oxford*
105. Blenheim Palace, *Woodstock*
106. Magdalen College, *Oxford*
107. New College, *Oxford*
108. Nuneham Courtenay, *Oxford*
109. Oxford Botanic Garden, *Oxford*
110. Rousham House, *Steeple Aston*
111. Shotover Park, *Forest Hill with Shotover*
112. Stonor, *Henley-on-Thames*

BEDFORDSHIRE
113. Woburn Abbey, *Woburn*
114. Wrest Park, *Silsoe*

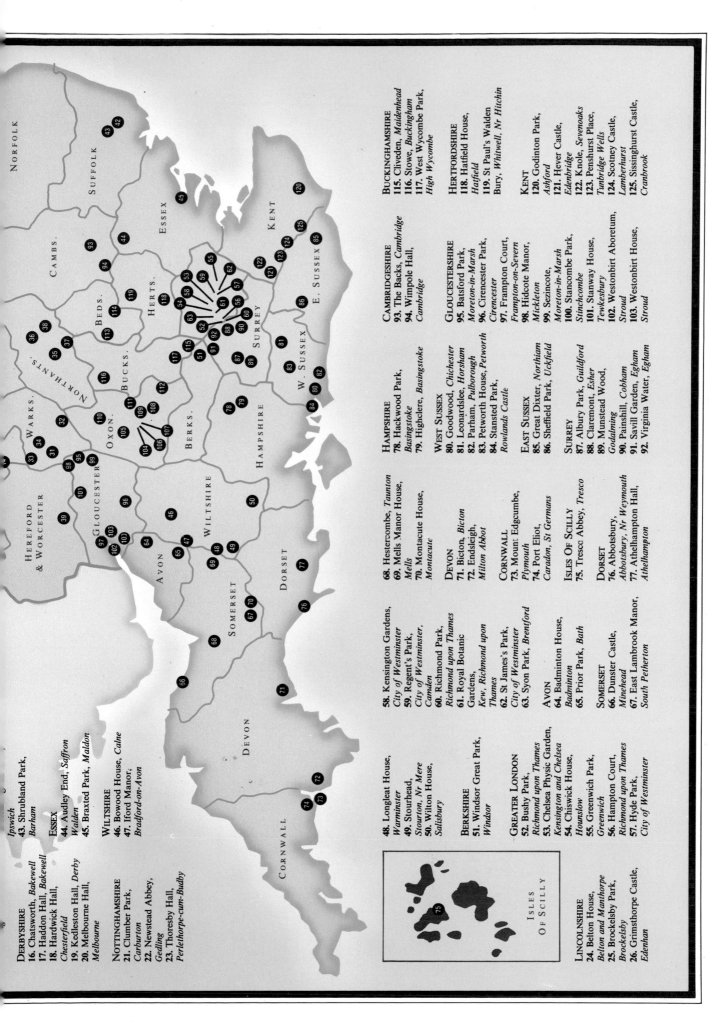

A SHORT BIBLIOGRAPHY

• • •

GARDEN HISTORY

Batey, Mavis, *Oxford Gardens*, 1982

Boniface, Priscilla, *The Garden Room*, 1982

Brown, Jane, *Gardens of a Golden Afternoon*, 1985

Coats, Alice M., *Flowers and their Histories*, 1968

Desmond, Ray, *Bibliography of British Gardens*, 1984

Elliott, Brent, *Victorian Gardens*, 1986

Fish, Margery, *We Made a Garden*, 1956

Forsyth, Alastair, *Yesterday's Gardens*, 1983

Green, David, *Gardener to Queen Anne*, 1956

Hadfield, Miles, *A History of British Gardening*, 1960, 1969

Harvey, John H., *Early Nurserymen*, 1974

Harvey, John H., *Mediaeval Gardens*, 1981

Hunt, John Dixon, and Willis, Peter, *The Genius of the Place*, 1975

Hunt, Peter, ed., *The Shell Gardens Book*, 1964

Hussey, Christopher, *English Gardens and Landscapes 1700–1750*, 1967

Jekyll, Gertrude, and Elgood, George, *Some English Gardens*, 1904

Jekyll, Gertrude, and Weaver, Lawrence, *Gardens for Small Country Houses*, 1913

Johnson, George W., *A History of English Gardening*, 1829, repr. *c.* 1978

[Loudon, J.C.], *In Search of English Gardens: the Travels of J. C. Loudon and his wife Jane*, ed. Boniface P., 1987

Newton, Norman T., *Design on the Land*, 1981

Rackham, Oliver, *Trees and Woodland in the British Landscape*, 1978

Sackville-West, Vita, *The Garden*, 1946

Scott-James, Anne, and Lancaster, Osbert, *The Pleasure Garden*, 1977

Stroud, Dorothy, *Capability Brown*, 1975

Taylor, Christopher, *The Archaeology of Gardens*, 1983

Thacker, Christopher, *The History of Gardens*, 1979, 1985

Thacker, Christopher, *The Enchanting Paths of Paradise*, 1989

Thomas, Graham Stuart, *Gardens of the National Trust*, 1979

[Tipping, Avray], *Gardens Old and New*, pub. *Country Life*, *c.* 1910

Weaver, Sir Lawrence, *Houses and Gardens by Sir Edwin Lutyens*, 1925

Willis, Peter, *Charles Bridgeman*, 1977

A principal source for material on gardens and their history lies in back numbers of certain periodicals – *Country Life*; *The Garden*; *Garden History*; the *Journal of Garden History*.

The English Heritage *Registers of Parks and Gardens . . . in England* may be obtained from: English Heritage Stores, room 32, Building 1, Vision Way, Victoria Rd, South Ruislip, Middlesex HA4 0NZ. Each county volume £3.50 inc p&p; Greater London £4.00.

TRAVELS AND MEMOIRS REFERRED TO IN THIS BOOK

D'Arblay, Mme, *Diary and Letters*, 4 vols, 1842

Blathwayt, William and John, *Diary . . . 1703*, ed. Hardwick, N., 1977

[Byng, John], *The Torrington Diaries*, ed. C.B. Andrews, 4 vols, 1934–38

Defoe, Daniel, *A Tour through England and Wales*, intr. Cole, G.D.H., 2 vols, (Everyman), n.d.

Evelyn, John, *Diary*, ed. Bray, W., 2 vols, 1945

Fiennes, Celia, *The Journeys*, ed. Morris, C., 1947

Kielmansegge, Count F., *Journal of a Journey to England . . . 1761–62*, 1902

Leigh, Dr C., *Natural History of Lancashire, Cheshire and the Peak*, 1700

Montagu, Elizabeth, *Correspondence . . . 1720 to 1761*, ed. Climenson, E.J., 2 vols, 1902

Moritz, C.P., *Travels in England in 1782*, 1924

Pococke, Dr Richard, *The Travels*, ed. Cartwright, J.J., 2 vols, 1888–89

Shenstone, William, *Letters*, ed. Williams, M., 1939

Taylor, John, *A New Discovery by Sea*, 1623, in vol. 3, Hindley, C., *The Old Book Collector's Miscellany*, 3 vols, 1872–3

Thoresby, Ralph, *Diary*, ed. Hunter, J., 2 vols, 1830

Vanbrugh, John, *Works*, ed. Webb, G., 4 vols, 1928

Walpole, Horace, 'Journal of Visits to Country Seats', ed. Toynbee, P., *Walpole Society*, vol. XVI, 1928

Young, Arthur, *Tours in England and Wales*, 1932

INDEX